Mirror to Goa

Donna J. Young

© By Donna J. Young
Edited by Victor Rangel-Ribeiro

Co-published in 2009 by

Saligão 403511 Goa, India. http://goa1556.goa-india.org, goa1556@gmail.com
+91-832-2409490
(Goa,1556 is an alternative publishing venture, named after the year of the accidental arrival of Asia's first Gutenberg-inspired printing press in Goa. Today, more than ever, Goa needs a voice to understand itself and articulate its priorities)

and

BROADWAY BOOK CENTRE

Ashirwad, 18th June Rd, Panjim 403001 Ph/fax 6647038.
http://broadwaybooksgoa.com
Project coordination by Frederick Noronha.
Cover design by Bina Nayak http://www.binanayak.com.
Cover photographs: FN http://photosfromgoa.notlong.com
Printed and bound in India by Rama Harmalkar, 9326102225
Typeset using LγX, http://www.lyx.org Text set in Palatino, 11 point.
ISBN 978-81-905682-1-0

Other publications of Goa,1556: SONGS OF THE SURVIVORS *(recollections by Goans in Burma, edited by Yvonne Vaz-Ezdani, 2007);* IN BLACK AND WHITE: INSIDERS' STORIES ABOUT THE PRESS IN GOA *(2008);* GIRLS IN GREEN *(alumni writings from St Mary's, Mapusa, 2008);*PICTURE-POSTCARD POVERTY: UNHEARD VOICES, FORGOTTEN ISSUES FROM RURAL GOA *(*NOV. 2008*);* MEDIEVAL GOA *by Dr Teotonio R de Souza (2009);* ANOTHER GOA *by Frederick Noronha (Nov 2009);* THE ART OF COCONUT CRAFT *by Vijaydatta Lotlikar (Dec 2009) .*
See http://goa1556books.notlong.com or http://goa1556.goa-india.org

---

Price: Rs 295 (hb) Rs. 195 (pb) in India.

*In dedication to the late James Heitzman (1950-2008),
my friend and mentor,
and to the late Dr. Camila Ribeiro da Costa (1914-2004),
who graciously allowed me to stay in her home and
assisted me with my research.*

Contents

A word of thanks — vi

1 Introduction — 1

2 Understanding Goa — 19

3 Identity, in transition — 32

4 Choosing a tongue — 53

5 Expats, and home — 71

6 Changing identity — 90

7 References — 96

8 Goa in creative writing — 102

Index — 164

A word of thanks

I WOULD like to express my gratitude to the many people whose assistance was crucial in completing this work.

My research began when I contacted Frederick Noronha. He quickly gave me the email address of his friend, writer Victor Rangel-Ribeiro. Victor and I quickly became friends, and he sent me numerous emails advising me of books to read and other sources that would be crucial for my research. We also sent emails back and forth discussing Goans and Goan identity.

Another Goan who assisted me through emails is Professor Peter Nazareth. He gave me advice on which novels to read and which authors' works it would be helpful for me to analyse.

When I decided to go to Goa, Victor Rangel-Ribeiro arranged to have me stay with his wonderful sister, the late Dr. Camila Ribeiro da Costa, and her husband Frank da Costa. Dr. Camila made arrangements for me to meet the people with whom I needed to talk, and also arranged for me to have access to all of the documents that were essential to this thesis. Frank and I had numerous discussions about Goa. He patiently explained everything to me and gave me newspaper articles, magazines, and books about Goa. Dr. Camila and Frank's son, Carlos, and his wife Rita, assisted me by driving me to many of the places I needed to visit. They were my tour guides and I am grateful for all of the time they spent with me because this was my first time in

Goa and I would have been lost without them. Without the assistance of the Ribeiro-da Costa family, I would not have been able to conduct my research.

I also want to thank some of Dr. Camila's friends who also were essential in assisting me. Prajal Sakhardande from Dhempe College spent the day with me, showing me Old Goa and other historical sites including a wonderful museum at the Rachol Seminary. Writer Margaret Mascarenhas invited me into her home and we discussed her book *Skin*. Percival Noronha also invited me into his home and shared his lecture notes with me.

I also wish to thank the Xavier Center for Historical Research and the Director of the Archives in Panjim. The staff at both places helped me locate the documents I needed, and saved me precious time.

I also want to thank my family for their unending support and encouragement. My mother went beyond the call of duty by accompanying me to Goa, even though she does not like spicy Indian food. She quickly fell in love with Goa and its people and wishes to return. In addition, I wish to thank my daughter, Jennifer, who encouraged me not to give up – even though it was hard at times because of poor health.

In addition, I want to thank the History Department at Georgia State University, especially the late James Heitzman and Dr. David McCreery. They were always available, supportive, and patient with me even when my health problems interfered.

And finally, I wish to thank Frederick Noronha again for assisting me in republishing this work, back where it should be read, dissected and debated – in Goa. A special thanks to Victor Rangel-Ribeiro for his meticulous editing of the manuscript, and for writing the foreword. I also wish to thank many other Goans who are not named here. Although I am a foreigner, they were happy and appreciative to learn that I am writing about Goa, and they opened their homes

A WORD OF THANKS

and hearts to me.

Donna J. Young,
Tucson, Arizona
October 2009

Chapter 1

Introduction

THE ISSUE of what constitutes Goan identity has baffled us now for some decades, perhaps because Goan identity must naturally be as fluid, as porous, and as amorphous as Goa's borders have been down the centuries.

Two millennia ago, that portion of the Konkan coast of which Goa is a part was known to the ancients as Aparanta, the Land Beyond the End. Its boundaries grew or shrank depending on the fortunes of war and which dynasty happened to be ruling where at that particular moment in time. But while we present-day Goans proudly lay claim to Aparanta as part of our heritage, the ancient Aparantans had no idea that this far into the future we would co-opt them as Goans.

Then, gradually, the name began to coalesce; a land called Gova and a city named Govapuri eventually emerged out of the mists of history. Goa itself only came to the world's attention after 1510, when the renegade sea captain Timoja invited Afonso de Albuquerque to sail with him up the Mandovi River so they could jointly teach the Sultan of Bijapur a lesson.

It is precisely for this reason that one of the most respected Goan figures of my generation, the author philosopher theologian architect muralist Sanskrit scholar Konkani protagonist folklorist and retired professor Jose Pereira, staunchly believes that Goan identity, far from being rooted in Aparanta, could only have begun with the Portuguese conquest of Goa, since until then Goa as a distinct entity "did not exist".

Pereira argues that Goa itself was a Portuguese military and administrative creation. So the captured city of Ela first became Goa, then "Golden Goa", and with the passing of centuries became Old Goa, yielding pride of place to Nova (New) Goa.

But history has ways of exacting its own revenge, and just as Portuguese military forces had overwhelmed the defenders of Ela between dawn and sunset on November 25, 1510, so did Indian armed forces overwhelm Goa's Portuguese defenders in a few hours on December 18 and 19, 1961. Only this time around there was no massacre, the world witnessed no four days of horror during which people were put to the sword or burnt alive in the places of worship in which they had sought refuge. For the Bijapuris as for the Portuguese who followed them in defeat, one might say: *sic transit gloria mundi*.

In the half-century that has passed since then, we Goans once again have had to decide, as our ancestors had to in 1510, just who we ourselves are, and where we are headed. "I was born legally a Portuguese in colonial Goa without my choice in February 1947 (while the rest of the country was on the threshold of independence)," the historian Teotonio R. de Souza wrote recently. "I became an Indian without my choice by a legislative process which followed the expulsion of the Portuguese regime. Our personal identity is greatly shaped by such unchosen developments of the collective history. Mine was no exception and some important life decisions became dependent upon the best available opportunities, but hardly of my choice."

WHILE IT IS easy for us to recognise a fellow-Goan, it is far more difficult to identify a common Goan identity. Those of us who live overseas usually have little difficulty in spotting another Goan in a crowd, either in bustling Times Square in New York or in a packed subway car deep in the bowels of London, or Lisbon, or Paris.

Physical features, skin colour, personal mannerisms, and — at close quarters — hearing a tone of voice and patterns of speech, all help in assessing whether or not the individual we are looking at is one of us. If confirmation is needed, a question asked in Konkani will provide the answer — sometimes. We need to remember that not all Goans speak Konkani, and also that not all Konkani speakers are Goan. But even assuming that the person we meet is a Goan, the question of his identity is something else again. Identity is more than skin deep; it is in part a state of mind. How does that individual regard himself?

João da Veiga Coutinho, the now reclusive Goan intellectual who decades ago transplanted himself into the United States, has much to say about Goan identity in his thought-provoking book, *A Kind of Absence: Life in the Shadow of History*. In a chapter titled "Thinking About History" he writes:

> At a gathering of immigrants newly settled in North America the question was debated: Is there a distinctive Goan personality? Almost immediately a rift appeared along the fault line dividing generations.
>
> Yes, a hybrid of East and West, a mixture of all the cultures that once dominated our ancestors. What is our culture anyway? Song and dance, food, caste, religion. An authoritarian culture, oppressive of women and the young.
>
> Goans are like coconuts, ventured someone, brown outside, white inside.
>
> There is really no Goan identity, another declared, only expediency, survival techniques.

Chameleon-like adaptability. Some Indian elements westernized, some western elements Indianized. Attachment to the land. Sentimental nostalgia.

No no not so! What is it to be Goan? Warmth, hospitality, family ties, a passion for excellence. The village is the heart of Goan culture. Goan youth abroad are completing the gradual loss of identity begun by their elders.... They wanted to be English or something... would not be found cooking Goan, wearing Indian clothes.... We must look for our roots in India.

But... look at colonial history!... look what they did! What options did our ancestors have?

...Other questions were asked: is religion the decisive factor in Goan identity? Is the Portuguese colonial legacy? If so, what is that legacy? Does the mere fact of having been born in Goa or of Goan stock endow one with a Goan identity? Is there a Goan past, a history common to all Goans?

Those of us who are of a certain age have all known, I think, Goan families who spent their entire lives within our frontiers and went to their graves not speaking or knowing even a word of Konkani; they spoke Portuguese instead. To their thinking, Konkani was for the servants; they themselves identified totally with the Portuguese. And there were other families, like mine, where my siblings and I grew up trilingual, speaking Portuguese, Konkani and English with equal facility.

Yet, language became a tool in the hands of the conqueror: in school and by fiat, we were taught the Portuguese language and Portuguese history to the utter neglect of our own language and our own history. At age 9, I knew some details of Portugal's defeat of the Spaniards at the battle of Aljubarrota, which took place some 4,000 miles from our shores and 540 years before I was born, but was taught nothing at all about the Sepoy Mutiny of 1895, and the Rane Rebellion that followed immediately after; yet, the mutiny and rebellion took place just a few miles from our house, and my own father and my maternal grandfather Hipolito Caetano Pinto were both involved in some of the events, but on opposing sides. In spite of Hipolito's nativist stand, I remember as a child standing stiffly at attention with the rest of our Boy Scout troop in Saligao and proudly singing "Heroes of the sea! Noble people, valiant and immortal nation! Lift up once again the glory of Portugal!" Why — unless we had been brainwashed or had been born stupid or were too young to reason — would we Goans want to raise up again the military glory of Portugal, years after the Colonial Act had been passed, stripping us of our status and our rights and turning us into second-class, underprivileged colonials?

However, that was in the 1930s. How do we Goans think of ourselves today? Do we think of ourselves as a) Goans first? b) As Indians first? c) As Goans who are Indians? d) As Indians who happen to be Goans? e) As Goans who are also Portuguese by right? f) As Portuguese who happen to be Goan by accident of birth? I have no scientific survey to back me up, but conversations with friends and acquaintances over the years have convinced me that, if the question were asked today, a) and c) would come out on top, with e) and f) trailing far behind.

Veiga Coutinho points to how indoctrination by the Portuguese led some Goans in bygone times to identify themselves with the Portuguese, and look down on the rest of the population. He takes particular aim at the highly respected polymath Gerson da Cunha (1844-1900), a Goan icon if ever there was one. Veiga Coutinho quotes da Cunha as having written:

> The seminary of the Holy Faith was soon in working order, having admitted youths of diverse Asiatic and African races, which com-

prised '*Canarins, Decanis do Norte, Malavares, Chingalás, Bengalas, Pegus, Malayos, Jaos e Abexins*'. Those who have visited the Esplanade des Invalides during the late Paris exhibition will be able to realize the charm and interest attaching to such an anthropological collection of living specimens. Even the Roman Propaganda College does not hold such a curious agglomeration of various Oriental types.

Veiga Coutinho asks very pointed questions: seeing that Gerson da Cunha was himself a "Canarim", how was he able to distance himself from the "Canarins" who were admitted to the Seminary of the Holy Faith, and how was he able to describe fellow Asians as "an anthropological collection of living specimens, a curious agglomeration of various Oriental types"? Veiga Coutinho reasons that Gerson da Cunha "had identified himself with the master, to whom he spiritually belonged and hoped to imitate. His mind had been remade in the master's image." Simply put, he belonged to the brainwashed generation.

Veiga Coutinho next tackles the writings of Fr. Gabriel Saldanha, the historian from Mapusa, who in 1892 was spending part of each day teaching Latin to one Oscar Rangel Ribeiro, who was destined to be my father but was at the time only 11 years old. In an imaginary "Conversation with the dead," João asks the scholar priest why, in writing the history of Goa, "you repeatedly say 'our' soldiers fought, 'our' armies invaded 'our' enemies, 'our' forces defended 'our' empire."

And the priest replies, "I realize we are not the Portuguese, but we are Portuguese. At least we were in my time. We were proud of being Portuguese."

Although Veiga Coutinho has put words in the dead priest's mouth, the sentiments that are expressed ring true given the context of those times: that nineteenth-century generation of Goan intellectuals took great pleasure in flinging their status as Portuguese in the face of the rulers in Lisbon, and also of the *descendentes* and *mestiços* who looked down on them in Goa itself: "We may be brown-skinned, but by law we are as Portuguese as you!"

One striking example: When in 1896, in the wake of the sepoy mutiny and the Rane rebellion, Governor Rafael de Andrade had unleashed a reign of terror on the local population, our representative in Portugal, Constancio Roque da Costa, anonymously wrote and published a series of articles called "Letters to His Highness Dom Afonso from a Portuguese." It is not just that being a Portuguese carried that much more weight; being a Goan patriot would have put the writer under suspicion of being a rebel sympathiser.

More than a hundred years have passed since Constancio Roque claimed to be a Portuguese in order to better stand up for Goa, and in that time the Portuguese and the British Empires have both ended up on the dust heap of history. Yet there are still some Goans around today who claim to be Portuguese; many of them do it out of a sense of genuine conviction; with others, however, it is a matter of political or racial motivation: not that they love Portugal more, but that they love India much less.

Jose Pereira, as we have seen, regards Goa as being largely a Portuguese creation; it follows therefore that Goan identity owes much to the Portuguese conquest and to Portuguese influence. Teotonio de Souza sees the identity issue differently and, I think, more clearly: "The origins of the Goan identity precede the arrival of the Portuguese," he said in a paper delivered at the roundtable on Goan identities held during Lusotopie's fourth meeting, February 29, 1999, "but four and a half centuries of colonial rule have left their mark." But in another paper he uses blunter language still: "...After nearly four and a half centuries of intense and sustained batterings of the Portuguese law, church rituals and Inquisition threats on a small enclave, Goans could not escape adopting overt and covert cultural habits that distinguish them from the rest of the inhabitants of the subcontinent."

What is left unsaid here is that, if any benefit at all accrued to Goans as the result of the Portuguese conquest and the batterings that followed, it is the Goan Catholic minority that benefited; the Hindu majority suffered grievous psychological harm, first by being under threat for their beliefs, then from seeing their temples forcibly destroyed, their priests kept in exile, and their mother tongue banned, and finally from the community itself being sidelined and disfranchised for decades. One can therefore reasonably assume, that as the result of Portuguese rule, a Goan Hindu identity came to exist that differs, in some aspects at least, from that of the Goan Catholic.

I would like to point out here that despite Portugal's long and determined attempts to impose a Portuguese culture on Goa, once Goans began to emigrate *en masse* to Bombay in search of a university education and well-paying jobs, we became exposed to liberal ideas and to India's push to independence; the more deeply we breathed in the heady winds of freedom, the more tenuous became Portugal's grip on our hearts and minds.

That this happened even before Liberation can be seen from a report that the Portuguese geographer Orlando Ribeiro sent to Salazar after being sent on a mission to Goa in 1956; Teotonio de Souza, the noted historian and former Director of the Xavier Centre of Historical Research in Alto Porvorim, quotes from it in a chapter he wrote for the recently published book, *Goa: Aparanta – Land Beyond the End*:

> Among all Portuguese territories I have known, Goa appears to me to be the least influenced by the Portuguese, less influenced than Guinea, which was pacified in 1912! Our language is widely ignored, the local society is alien and indifferent to us, at times even hostile to our presence; Portuguese influence is very scanty; Goa is

like a cancerous growth on the body of a reviving Hinduism; I was very disappointed in Goa.

Things changed even faster after Liberation; with the founding of the Xavier Centre of Historical Research in 1977, and the establishment of Goa University seven years later, the Goa Archives began to be mined for purposes other than the glorification of Portugal. And where the question for some individuals might once have been, "Is there a Goan identity, distinct from a Portuguese identity," now a new question arose: "Is there a Goan identity, distinct from an Indian identity?"

Peter Nazareth reminded me recently that in East Africa, for the first half of the twentieth century, the ruling Whites looked on Goans who settled there as a people to be set apart from other Indians. This allowed for some subtle distinctions to be made in discriminatory practices, so that Goans eventually came to provide the underpinnings of the British colonial administrative services. Peter himself felt quite differently. "At first I thought of myself as African," he told me. "My first play, broadcast by the BBC in England, had African characters in it but no Goans. It was an African colleague who asked me a pointed question: 'Why don't you put some Goan characters into your writing?' And so I did."

"Not to deny my Indianness," Peter continued, "but now I think of myself as being a Goan first, as well as being an Indian. Being a Goan automatically makes me an Indian; being an Indian would not necessarily make me a Goan." That is a point very well taken.

Much before Liberation, the talented but neglected poet Joseph Furtado also believed there was a distinction between Goans and other Indians. He complained in the 1920s that his better-known contemporaries, Paulino Dias and Nascimento Mendonça, were "more Indian than Goan", basing his criticism on the fact that he himself, from 1927 on, wrote "many serious verses in English on Goan matters", while they did not.

Peregrino da Costa, writing in Portuguese about the expansion of the Goan diaspora across the world, also claimed that Goans are different from "the rest of India", but for quite a different reason; I have freely translated the passage as follows:

a people of fewer than 600,000 souls
possessing a special mentality
resulting from the superimposition of the European spirit
on the Indian,
forms as it were a spiritual unity and a social community
different from the rest of India.

Here again we have the bald statement that what makes the Goan different from his fellow-Indian is the fact that he possesses "a special mentality", as the result of a supposedly superior "European spirit" having been superimposed on the Indian! And the statement comes not from a Portuguese, but from a Goan!

In a special chapter on "Goan Identity and the Diaspora" written for *Goa: Aparanta – Land Beyond the End*, the late Chandrakant Keni argued that a fusion of "geographical endowments, historical developments, and cultural, linguistic and religious heritage interacting upon one another ...go to shape the identity of a people, setting them apart even while they remain an integral part of the mainstream." Together these factors help create "a distinctive way of life, a unique folklore, art and craft, dance and music, distinctive cuisine, unique architecture, and overall a different cadence and rhythm of life."

Indeed, while the centuries of Portuguese occupation helped shape Goan identity to a great extent, Goa's "geographical endowments" played a significant role as well, both before and after their arrival.

Mountains have an insulating effect on a people, and for hundreds of years the great and deeply forested arc of the Western Ghats, though barely a thousand metres high, cut us off from the hinterland of India, allowing the inhabitants of Goa to develop a culture and a way of life distinct from that prevailing in the hinterland, just as the mountains in Great Britain helped the Scots and the Welsh set themselves apart from the English, and a mountain range in the Iberian Peninsula helped the Portuguese assert themselves as a nation vis-à-vis the Spaniards.

At the same time, the joint estuary of the Mandovi and Zuari rivers, opening out on to the Arabian Sea, provided both a gateway and an early point of entry between Goa and the rest of the world. For two millennia, some historians say, the natural sheltered harbours on these two rivers drew traders not just from the Horn of Africa, but from nations bordering on the Mediterranean, and from peoples to the north and south of us. Thus our rivers and the ocean that laps at our shores began impacting on our history long before the *naus* and *caravelas* first sailed into our waters, and have continued to impact on us long after those sturdy ships furled their sails for ever.

While many have commented on the importance and extent of Goa's seaborne links, it was left to Teotonio to comment on the significance of the escalation that occurred once Albuquerque struck: "The integration of Goa into the Portuguese eastern empire after 1510," Teotonio writes, "catapulted it into an unforeseen scale of operations. As headquarters of an early modern European empire from 1530, Goa exposed its inhabitants very early to the challenges of modern globalization."

Goa, pioneering in globalization in 1530? Now that's a profound insight!

As for Goa's linguistic heritage, early missionaries among the Portuguese realized its importance, and pioneered in codifying the language and publishing sacred texts in Konkani; however, official policy later turned to banning the use of the vernacular, both in public and in our schools. Ironically, Konkani not only survived but enriched itself by borrowing hundreds of Portuguese terms and idioms, incorporating them in ways that suited Goan patterns of speech.

So the move to expunge Konkani failed; Chandrakant Keni points out that "even Goans who fled to safety in regions where different languages were spoken took care to hold on to their mother tongue, and many of their descendants speak Konkani to this day. This would not have happened if Konkani had not been at the very core of their Goan identity." Thus, to Keni, Konkani is a strong force unifying Goans and their descendants, including those who have settled in disparate parts of India.

Jose Pereira, on the other hand, feels that Goan identity in the new India faces the threat of fragmentation, because of the strong challenge posed to Konkani by Marathi, which he says has been and continues to be more successful than our own native mother tongue in every field of endeavour. It does not help that the Konkani movement is itself fragmented, with protagonists of Devanagari and Romi scripts at each other's throats.

Keni also has an anecdote about the importance of food as a marker of identity. He describes how, at the time of the Opinion Poll, "a scholar from Goa, a staunch advocate of Marathi, visited Mumbai as the guest of a Marathi institution. He noticed that people from different states and regions had created their own cultural islands; he was especially surprised that even Goan Hindus – and not just Goan Catholics, who he believed had been brainwashed by the Portuguese and by missionaries – did not intermix with the dominant Maharashtrian community, even though they had mastered the language and considered themselves culturally Maharashtrians. He tried to impress on them the need to assimilate, as otherwise they would be treated as strangers.

"However, the Goan scholar himself, who as a VIP was being served the choicest Maharashtrian delicacies, found he could not relish them for long. After the first two days he felt a nausea developing when meals were served, and wondered whether something had gone wrong with his digestive system. One evening he came across a restaurant with a signboard advertising a 'Gomantak Rice Plate'. It reminded him of his normal diet and he decided to eat there. He came out a totally changed man, having realized that not merely the fish curry and rice, but even the vegetarian food prepared by Goans is different from Maharashtrian food. Even our food, he found, has a different identity."

I recently telephoned João da Veiga Coutinho at his new home outside Albuquerque, in New Mexico, and asked him if he had changed his views on Goan identity. The spry 91-year-old thinker promptly asked me what my own views were. I said I believed Goans had several identities depending on history, social circumstances and family upbringing, but that a Portuguese layer had been added to many of us through a process I could only compare to brainwashing. "And yet," João retorted, "may I remind you of what Orlando Ribeiro told Salazar: 'Goans are the least Portuguese of all the people in the overseas provinces.'" Then João chuckled and said, "We are chameleon-like."

So many elements go to make up Goan identity that we are able to adapt to all manner of circumstances, and so survive. Professor Peter Nazareth of the University of Iowa believes it is a direct result of Portuguese rule: "Once you have two cultures in you, you can deal with many more." He feels this puts Goans in an advantageous position in that they can interpret one culture to another; they become, in his words, "cultural brokers".

Naturally, this applies particularly to Goans in the diaspora. In one essay, Prof. Nazareth writes about his own heritage:

> John [his brother] and I were born in Uganda and were African and not African; Indian and not Indian; and Goan and yet not Goan because our mother was born in Malaya. Yet I, Peter,

am a classic Goan in being a cultural broker, as when I have written about three individuals from three different cultures – Ishmael Reed (African American), Andrew Salkey (Jamaican) and Francis Ebejer (Maltese) – all in one book.

He points out that African writers regard him as an African writer and critic on African literature, the Malaysians regard him as a Malaysian, while he himself is a Goan, an Indian happily ensconced in the heartland of America. In that heartland, Peter is embraced as an American.

Chandrakant Keni's great fear, shared by very many Goans, is that our identity will be lost as hordes of outsiders – the much resented and detested *bhaile* – pour in across the border to work and then to settle in our midst. My own observation has been that many of these newcomers quickly learn Konkani; they appreciate and assimilate our culture, and integrate themselves quickly into the Goan milieu. There is no doubt, however, that a continuous influx of migrants will tip the balance that now exists between the established image of a Goa *dourada* – a golden Goa that has been almost entirely shaped by Portuguese culture and Western civilization – and the emerging image of a Goa Indica, a term invented by the British anthropologist Caroline Ifeka to highlight India's long contribution to Goan identity.

Our own famous Goa-friendly anthropologist, Robert S. Newman, endorses Ifeka's view. In *Of Umbrellas, Goddesses & Dreams*, his remarkable book of essays on Goan culture and society, Newman points out that Goa "comprises a compact geo-cultural region with a common language and history", then adds:

> There is also a basic foundation of common culture – Goa Indica – the image never developed, the identity never grasped to the bosom of the mainly Brahmin, Westernized intellectuals. Goa Indica, it appears to me, is the ideal instrumental identity for Goa, the way in which the major-

ity of Goans can be bound together for political stability, providing in addition, the avenue for the absorption of the 'newcomers' who are 'non-Goans' today but whose children must surely be Goan tomorrow, for Goa has absorbed outsiders before and still managed to maintain its own identity. The common Goan culture, even today, under strong pressure from Western media and education, still exists. The majority of Goans participate in that culture, even if they have never written about it.

Caste is perhaps the most pernicious feature of that common culture; it has not only survived Catholicism but now permeates it like a malignant virus. Teotonio lays it on the line: "No discussion on Goan identity can be complete by ignoring the caste system that dogs Goan society.... Despite all the *haute couture* and other external shenanigans that Goans have acquired over time and made them presentable global citizens, Goan identity has yet to break out of its caste shell."

One element we have considered only in passing is religion. Most of all, Goan identity lies rooted in our realization that Catholics and Hindus alike share a Hindu past; that centuries ago we shared a common faith, and worshipped the village deity in the village temple. That relationship did not change when some of us were converted to Christianity, nor did it end when our temples were destroyed; we continued to be brothers and sisters.

It is for this reason that a bond exists between Goan Catholics and Goan Hindus that does not seem to exist in the rest of India. Most Goan Catholic families know who their ancient village deities were, and where the temples were relocated once temple destruction became accepted policy. Some Goan Catholics still pay annual tribute to the old family temple, in money and in kind – oil for heating and cooking, a couple of roosters, a basketful of coconuts, what have you. To balance this, devout Hindu worshippers also feel free to walk into Catholic churches and chapels while Mass or some other religious service is in progress, to touch the feet of a saint or the Virgin Mary, to say a silent prayer or leave an offering.

The pull of the family deity is so strong that for centuries Goan Hindus who live outside Goa's borders have made it a practice to go home to worship in the family temple. While Goan Catholics do not feel the same urge to visit Goa in order to go to their village church, they do feel the pull to visit their family home and village.

Sometimes the desire involves making Goa their final resting place. I remember that on the several occasions that my aging father left Goa to visit my sister's family and mine in the United States, we pressed him to settle down with us, and his answer was always the same, a refusal softened by a gentle smile: "Much though I'd like that, I want to leave my bones in Goa." He eventually did, in Porvorim, at age 90.

The longing of the Goan exile to be reunited with the motherland even in death has often been set in words, but nowhere as passionately, I believe, as was done by my oldest sister on January 1, 1961. Leonor Rangel Ribeiro at the time was serving as a UN adviser to the Government of Colombia in Bogota, and wrote a poem expressing her oneness with Goa and her thoughts on the possibility of dying abroad. I will quote just the seven closing lines:

> *Toda essa harmonia de divino amor que é Goa*
> *Sou eu! ...*
> *E se um dia num país distante*
> *A Morte me ceifasse sem dó,*
> *Voltaria à terras de Goa,*
> *Voltaria nas asas do vento*
> *Mesmo como pó.*

Loosely translated, this reads:

> All this harmony of divine love that is Goa,
> It is me!
> And if one day in a distant land

> Death should cull me without mercy,
> I will return to the lands of Goa
> Will return on the wings of the wind
> Even as dust.

Having quoted the sage opinions of João da Veiga Coutinho, Jose Pereira, Peter Nazareth, Teotonio R. de Souza, and Robert S. Newman, and added a few of my own, I am reminded of the following quatrain from Edward Fitzgerald's translation of *The Rubáiyát of Omar Khayyám*:

> Myself when young did eagerly frequent
> Doctor and saint and heard great argument
> About it and about, but evermore
> Came out by the same door where in I went.

The American researcher Donna Young, aware perhaps of the danger of such an outcome, deliberately picked a different path in her quest for Goan identity: she chose to examine how we Goan writers write about ourselves, about our own people.

Instead of limiting herself to sounding out the views of just a few individuals, as I have done, she read deeply in the extant Goan literature in English, sifting through their content for clues. She rightly assumed that, though the word-portraits we produce in fiction might be couched in less scholarly and philosophical terms than some views I have quoted here, they might yet be more revealing of the true nature of Goan identity because they are heartfelt and intuitive.

Perhaps Ms. Young's research will also reveal that Goan identity, like the identity of so many peoples, really consists of a multiplicity of layers that history from time to time has fused together, and is now busy peeling apart. Teotonio has confessed that some of the layers "make me cry, due to the ambiguities and contradictions involved in the process of the historical growth of 'my people.'" I will cry along with Teotonio, and for the same reason; but Donna Young knows very well that the process of historical growth and identity change will continue, no matter how many tears Teotonio and I might shed

Victor Rangel-Ribeiro
Monroe, New Jersey, April 19, 2009.

Chapter 2

Understanding Goa

BECAUSE GOA, India, was a Portuguese colony for more than four hundred and fifty years; because it was incorporated into India as a territory in 1961; and because it became a separate state in 1987, there is an issue as to whether Goans have a separate identity, an Indian identity, a dual identity, or no identity at all.

Goa's location on the Arabian Sea has historically made it a strategic port. As a result, it has been subject to many influences through the centuries and the identity of the people has changed over time.

Its geographic location in a tropical climate with fertile land has made it attractive for agriculture. In recent times however, many Goans have been forced to leave the area for lack of economic opportunities. Because so many Goans and their descendants now live outside of Goa, an additional question that needs to be answered is: Who is a Goan?

In order to reach a conclusion on these issues it is necessary to examine the geography and history of Goa and also to examine Goans' own perceptions about themselves.

CHAPTER 2. UNDERSTANDING GOA
Geography, History

GOA is located on the western Indian coastline of the Arabian Sea about 300 miles (480 kms) south of Bombay (Mumbai). It shares a border with the state of Maharashtra to the north and northeast and with Karnataka to the south, east and southeast.

The state is administratively divided into two districts: North and South Goa. The major cities are the state capital Panaji (formerly called Panjim, Pangim or Nova Goa, and Ponnje in the local tongue Konkani), Margao, Vasco da Gama and Mapusa. The state is further divided into eleven talukas or administrative districts: Pernem, Bicholim, Sattari, Bardez and Tiswadi in North Goa, and Mormugao, Salcete, Sanguem, Ponda, Quepem and Canacona in South Goa.

Compared to other Indian states, Goa is small. It is only 62 miles (100 km) long and approximately 30 miles (48 km) wide. This small state, however, has three different geographical areas: the rugged slopes of the Sahyadri mountains, the midland region, and the coastal section. The mountainous region is famous for the Dudhsagar waterfall and is Goa's least populated area. It provides most of the state's fresh water and is the source of all of Goa's seven main rivers.

Two of the most important rivers, the Zuari and the Mandovi, cut across the center of the state, meeting to form a wide estuary which forms the westernmost dividing line between North Goa and South Goa.

The midland region is comprised of laterite plateaus approximately 40 to 350 feet in elevation. In the lower parts of the region there are many fruit and nut plantations. Most of Goa's Hindu population resides in this area because it was not conquered by the Portuguese until the late eighteenth century.

The coastal region is the best known area of Goa because

it is famous for its golden beaches and has become a popular tourist destination.

Goa is 745 miles (1200 kms) south of the Tropic of Cancer. Its climate is tropical and has only two seasons: the dry season and the monsoon. The dry season lasts six to eight months with temperatures ranging between 80 and 95 degrees during the day with low humidity; the monsoon season occurs between June and the end of September, when the state can receive up to 36 inches of rain during the month of July itself. Total annual rainfall averages 277 cms (109 inches). Travel is difficult during the rainy season and strong winds and high seas make the beaches and fishing off limits.

The population of Goa is approximately 1.4 million people. An estimated 66% are Hindus, 29% are Christians, and five per cent are Muslim; a few are Sikhs or belong to other religions. [1]

Statistics alone, however, do not explain the interesting religious blend that is found in Goa. In the early years of Portuguese rule, many Hindus converted to Christianity, some from conviction and others to retain their property rights or because they felt pressured. In some instances part of the family would move to areas outside Portuguese control while the other half of the family stayed in Portuguese Goa. From the time of the Portuguese conquest, many Goans have had family members of different religions.

Brahmin families converting to Catholicism retained their caste. Even today, Goans, both Christian and Hindu, in some areas observe the same festivals or at least pay their respects to the other faith. The festivals unite both faiths in the villages in celebration.

Goa's economy is predominately agricultural. Rice, fruits, coconuts, legumes, cashews and betel nuts are the state's major crops. Goa exports these products as well as spices, manganese, iron ore, bauxite, fish and salt. It man-

---

[1]Bradnock, Goa Handbook, 17.

ufactures fertilisers, sugar, textiles, chemicals, iron pellets, and pharmaceuticals.

The tourist industry has grown since the late 1960s, but particularly after the mid-1980s, when European charter tourists flew into Dabolim, first from Germany and later from other countries including the UK, Scandinavia and Russia. Tourism has now become an essential part of the Goan economy.

Historically, Goa has been known by many names such as Gove, Govapuri, and Gomant. Medieval Arabian geographers knew it as Sindabur or Sandabur.

Sometime in the Middle Stone Age, it was settled by Dravidian people, who later mixed with Aryan invaders about 1500 BC. Beginning about the first century AD, Goa's position on the Arabian Sea and its natural harbours made it an important international trading center. Goa was ruled by the Kadamba dynasty from around the ninth century AD to 1312 with its capital Govapuri on the banks of the Zuari river.

Muslim rulers from the Deccan region invaded the area and ruled it from 1312 to 1367. It was then annexed to the Hindu Vijayanagar empire and later conquered by the Muslim Bahmani dynasty.

The Bahmani and the Vijayanagar rulers throughout the fifteenth century fought over control of Goa and, in 1470, the Muslim general Mahmud Gawan finally drove out the Vijayanagars. Disputes divided the Bahamani empire, and the Muslim king of Bijapur became the region's ruler.

In 1510, the Portuguese attacked the city because they wanted Goa's ports in order to control access to the lucrative spice trade routes of India, Ceylon (Sri Lanka) and the East Indies (Indonesia).

At first, Alfonso de Albuquerque was able to conquer the city with little struggle. Some sources claim the Hindus invited the Portuguese in order to overthrow their Muslim rulers and then expected them to leave.

Three months later, the king of Bijapur returned with sixty thousand troops and drove out the Portuguese invaders. Albuquerque recaptured the city, and massacred the Muslims.

Goa was Portugal's first territorial possession in Asia. Within a few decades, the Portuguese then made Goa the capital of their empire in the East.

Albuquerque left almost untouched the customs of the communities in the islands in the Mandovi River, with the exception of abolishing *sati*, the practice of immolation of widows.

Soon after, however, laws passed in 1541 ordered the destruction of Hindu temples, banned Hindu rituals, and decreed that only those who were baptised could retain the rights to their land. In 1560 the Inquisition began almost two hundred years of religious persecution.

Severe punishment was inflicted upon the Christian converts, out of fear that continuation of their traditional lifestyle would weaken the new religion's hold over them. In an attempt to force Goans to speak Portuguese, in 1684 the governor banned the use of any indigenous language. The Konkani language, however, continued to be widely used in the home inspite of the Portuguese ban.

To escape the oppression caused by the Inquisition, many Hindus fled across the Mandovi and other rivers of the region, taking their Hindu religious objects with them; a number of the Christian converts fled to South India.

Many converts, however, remained and the Catholic Church's presence continued to grow without much apparent opposition.

By the middle of the sixteenth century, the religious orders of the Franciscans, Dominicans, Augustinians, and Jesuits had established many schools and hospitals. Construction of the Sè Cathedral (the largest in Asia) began in 1560;the Basilica of Bom Jesus (which contains the remains of St. Francis Xavier) was built between 1594 and 1605.

When Philip II of Spain became King of Portugal, Portugal lost its power and control over the Indian Ocean. The Dutch became so powerful that they drove the Portuguese out of South East Asia. They blockaded Goa in 1603, but did not succeed in taking it. Epidemics of cholera and other illnesses also contributed to Goa's decline. The Portuguese population in Goa decreased to the extent that Portugal sent criminals to Goa in order to boost its presence.

In the mid-eighteenth century, a series of reforms included the end of the Inquisition and confiscation of Jesuit property; still, Portugal's power base in Goa remained weak, and the Marathas were a constant threat. When, however, an Afghan army destroyed Maratha power at the battle of Panipat in 1761, the Portuguese turned the debacle into their own advantage by pushing Goa's frontiers all the way to the Ghats. Pernem, Ponda, Satari, Sanguem, Quepem and Canacona, along with Bicholim, which had been conquered earlier, were added to Goa and called the "New Conquests", to distinguish them from the areas that had long been under Portuguese rule. While Goa grew somewhat in size, Portugal's power in other parts of Asia continued to decline.

In the "New Conquests" the people remained mainly Hindu because the missionaries did not have the zeal to handle conversions after the end of the Inquisition. Since Portuguese clerics held all major church positions, there was also pressure to abolish racial discrimination within the Church.

In 1787, Goa experienced an important revolt against Portuguese authority. A group of priests met in the house of the Pinto family in Candolim and plotted to overthrow the government. Fifteen of the 47 conspirators in the Pinto Rebellion were arrested, tortured and executed. The rebellion helped to speed up the reforms to end racist policies that prevented Goans from holding positions of authority and power in the Catholic Church. During the Napoleonic Wars, Portugal itself was occupied by Napoleon's troops, and the

British occupied Goa from 1799 until 1813.

During the early nineteenth century, the Inquisition officially ended and church reforms were put in place to end racial discrimination. Panjim (now Panaji) was declared the capital in 1843.

For the next hundred years, Portugal clung on to its colony and administered it in a desultory manner. Beneath the surface, an independence movement slowly formed and gained ground after the First World War. Portugal's neutrality during the Second World War did not leave Goa unaffected by the events in Europe; it became an intelligence center used by both the British and the Germans.

At the end of World War II, when India achieved Independence, the Portuguese came under increasing pressure from India to cede Goa.

In response to this pressure, Portugal dispatched more than four thousand troops to try to retain the colony. Amongst Goans, there was little support for the issue one way or the other.

In 1955, *satyagrahis* from India attempted to enter Goa but were deported. More *satyagrahis* who tried to enter Goa were stopped by Portuguese troops. Minor skirmishes continued. At a demonstration in Margao, the police fired on an unarmed crowd, killing 32 people and injuring 225. Sporadic violence continued until Indian troops invaded Goa on December 18, 1961, ending four hundred and fifty one years of Portuguese rule in Goa in less than two days.

From 1961 until 1987, Goa, along with the former Portuguese enclaves of Daman and Diu, was a Union Territory. During this time, the transformation of Goa's almost medieval economy occurred. Dramatic changes in the infrastructure included the establishment of colleges and a university; bridges were built, roads paved, and electricity installed.

For example: in 1961 only three villages out of 374 had electricity; in 1980, 330 of them had electricity. And students no longer had to go to Bombay or Portugal to obtain a higher education.

During this time, there was much controversy over whether Goa should become a state rather than a territory of India, and whether Marathi or Konkani should become the official state language. There were heated arguments for both languages because some people felt that Goa should be joined to the State of Maharashtra. Although the issue continues to be raised, Goans chose to remain a separate entity (as against merger with Maharashtra) in a 1967 Opinion Poll. Goa became a State in 1987 and in 1992 Konkani became one of the official languages of India.

Although it is not one of India's poor states, Goa today is facing many problems. Because of its high unemployment, it is losing many educated adults while, at the same time, importing manual labor from other parts of India. Goans are leaving this state in record numbers to further their education or to work. They head to places like Kuwait and its neighbourhood (also called "The Gulf"), or England, to Canada, the U.S., and Australia; they plan to make money and hope to return to Goa with their wealth.

Tourism is having a significant impact on the economy, so much so that people jokingly refer to the state as "Touristan." The local hotels in northern Goa are giving way to large resort hotels and the beach areas are overrun by stalls selling crafts and a variety of touristy items made in other parts of India and hawked by non-Goans, including many Kashmiris.

Methodology, theories

PRESENTED here is an examination of the writings of Goan fiction writers and scholars. By analyzing their views on the issue of Goan identity, I hope to avoid the possible pitfalls of Orientalism, defined by Edward Said as "the idea of European identity as a superior one in comparison with all non-European peoples and culture."[2]

Using Western or non-Goan sources would create a Goan identity with a Western bias. In *Orientalism*, "knowledge of the Orient, because generated out of strength, in a sense creates the Orient, the Oriental and his world....The Oriental is something one judges... one studies and depicts, one disciplines ... or illustrates."[3] The assumption was that everything in the Orient was either inferior or needed to be studied by the West so that it could be corrected.

While sources such as government publications, statistics, and documents reveal a great deal about a society, there are other sources that many people overlook that reveal insights about Goans and their views on identity. These sources reveal all aspects of Goan life, especially social status, race, political, and social issues. An analysis of relevant literature – such as novels, plays, short stories, essays, and pamphlets – is presented for consideration. Additional sources including periodicals, interviews, internet sites, internet bulletin boards, and internet newspapers, provide current opinions on these topics.

All of the included literature is written in English, with the exception of *The Upheaval/Acchev*, which was translated from Konkani. The reason for not including literature written in Konkani or Marathi is the lack of English translations. The majority of the literature available to a non-Konkani and non-Marathi speaker is in English, and many speakers of those languages read and understand English. Very little is written in Portuguese, especially after Goa became part of India.

The use of translated works, if available, could potentially be a problem to use in determining how Goans perceive themselves. Translations are sometimes not accurate

---
[2]Said, *Orientalism*, 7.
[3]*ibid.*, 40.

and often the translator is influenced by his or her own identity. Edward Said points out that in Europe, in the nineteenth and early twentieth centuries, there was a large amount of literature about the Orient. It was called an "Orientalism renaissance." Said declares that:

> Suddenly it seemed to a wide variety of thinkers, politicians, and artists, that a new awareness of the Orient, which extended from China to the Mediterranean, had arisen. This awareness was partly the result of newly discovered and translated Oriental texts in languages like Sanskrit, Zend, and Arabic; it was also the result of a newly perceived relationship between the Orient and the West. [4]

Said suggests that Orientalists used translated texts in order to reinforce the opinion of the superiority of Europe or the West over the East.

In all of the sources analyzed, Goans are proud of their unique and complex identity. As ManoharRai Sardessai writes, "Nothing is simpler than being a Goan.... For God in his infinite sagacity has divided the world into two continents, Goa and the rest of the world: and the whole of humanity into two distinct races: Goans and non-Goans." John Hobgood feels that this "Goan celebration of self-worth is what any ethnic group will do that has a dynamic living culture."[5] Peter Nazareth notes:

> Goans are not used to seeing themselves in literature....they tend to think of it as gossip...they do not realize that [fiction writers] do not just write gossip reflecting the attitudes and perspectives of gossips; that much of the [writer's] work not only deals with colonial politics but also questions the hardness of some Goan traditions

---

[4]Said, *op.cit.*, 42.
[5]Hobgood, "Defining Goans," 15.

and the absence of love in Goans, an absence of
which if not followed by self-awareness leads to
the vacuum being filled by non-Goans.[6]

It is therefore through an examination of Goan literature and other writings by Goan authors that a different and more balanced perspective on Goan identity and its evolving nature is presented. While the views of non-Goan scholars can give an allegedly objective view of Goan identity, it is how Goans themselves view their own identity that gives a more complete viewpoint on the subject.

The difficulty in defining Goan identity is that it is a changing condition. Teotonio R. de Souza, a prominent Goan historian, believes:

[C]ultural identities are defined as transient
phases of identification. Even those identities
which appear well defined and presenting an appearance of permanency are subject to changing
shades of meanings and to gradual or fast transformations in their underlying contents.[7]

Goan identity has undergone many changes because it was a Portuguese colony for four-and-half centuries before it became a state of India. Goa never achieved its own independence and the people went through a long struggle in examining and exploring their identity.

Although it is claimed by some that Goans have no identity, a much stronger argument can be made that Goans have developed a dual Goan/Indian identity which is largely based upon their ties to India, a renewed interest in their heritage which includes the Konkani language, and the increased importance of the concept of the ancestral home to which they long to return.

Goan identity today is also greatly affected by the Diaspora. As more Goans are leaving Goa to live in countries all

---

[6]Nazareth, "End of Exile," 35.
[7]Souza, "Goan Identity," 2001.

over the world, the use of Konkani is decreasing and more Goans are writing in English. It is noteworthy that most Goans are emigrating to English-speaking countries such as Great Britain, Canada, Australia, or the United States.

Most Goans study English in school, and it is widely spoken in Goa. Writing in English is therefore not only an influence of the expatriates' newly adopted countries, but it is also a way to ensure that the descendants of Goans will have parts of their culture preserved.

Literature written in English is more likely to be read by Goans, both at home and abroad. Peter Nazareth explains the reason this literature is important, especially to those who are expatriates:

> What does Goan – and other relevant – literature have to offer Goans, particularly those growing up in Canada and cut off from Goan history? Scholars have recently written much about centuries of Goan history, and it is important for us to know it. Thanks to colonialism, most of us only know about the history of European empires.... Goan literature shows Goans what is imprinted in them by a history they do not know, and shows them further how to recognize it, draw from it or draw it out, and then to make rational choices.[8]

The complexity of the issue of Goan identity can be resolved by examining various aspects of Goan culture through the eyes of Goans themselves.

Their long history of Portuguese domination has left an indelible mark on their culture. Superimposed on the culture, since 1961, is an Indian/Hindu influence which is supported by some Goans and rejected by others.

Because Goa has a diverse cultural population composed of three different religions, different social classes, and exiles

---

[8]Nazareth, *op.cit.*, 36-37.

returning home, the state is always going to be comprised of people with differing opinions. Despite these differences, there is a common background of being a former colony of Portugal.

The language differences have largely been resolved in spite of being resurrected periodically by Marathi supporters for political purposes. There exists a separate Goan identity as opposed to an Indian identity alongside a joint Goan-Indian identity that is evident in the current literature and is widely discussed by Goan writers in English.

Chapter 3

Identity, in transition

GOAN IDENTITY is an extremely complex issue. Even Goans themselves cannot agree on a definition of who is Goan. A.K. Priolkar states that he cannot define a Goan to his satisfaction. Not only is there the issue of who is considered Goan, but also the problem that the territory of Goa was enlarged when it was under Portuguese rule.

Does the definition of Goa only include the original territory of the island of Tiswadi or all of the land that was added by the Portuguese, and became a state after it joined India? Priolkar argues that Goa defines all of the land that the Portuguese conquered that later became the state of Goa.

The second issue the writer confronts, determining who is a Goan, is much harder to define than the borders of Goan territory.

Goans have long disputed amongst themselves whether they are Goan, Portuguese, or Indian. Priolkar states that even groups that claim to be Portuguese or Indian should still be considered Goan.

Without giving a reason, he finally decides that a Goan is "anyone, whatever his present whereabouts, whose forefathers have been domiciled in Goa, at anytime in history and who is aware of his connection and cherishes and values it."[1] In other words, this broad definition does not eliminate those of Goan descent or those who hold other citizenships being defined as Goan, especially in the literary community.

Goan identity is an issue that has often been debated in its literature. It is an important theme in the majority of Goan books and short stories written both by Goans who still continue to live in Goa and those who live abroad. The literature is intended for a Goan audience who understand the political debates and points of view of the characters. The major debates include whether Goans are Portuguese, Indian, or simply Goans, and whether they should use Marathi or Konkani as their official state language.

Karin Larsen's *Faces of Goa* states that Goan cultural identity does not remain static, it is constantly changing.

> "Culture is dynamic and is marked by the process of reinterpretation and syncretism. Reinterpretation is the process through which any element of culture undergoes a marked change."[2]

According to Larsen, Goans formed a new identity after the Portuguese conquered them. When they accepted the new ways of the Portuguese, other aspects of Goan society became more valued and traditional: the family home, social class, and gaining economic status. "[T]hose traits which may upset the stability of the culture will be rejected."[3]

Goans adopted some Portuguese culture, but never completely identified with the Portuguese. This separate identity, the tradition of maintaining the family home and increasing one's social status, caused the rise in the desire for self rule. While many authors who write about Goa's liberation focus on the twentieth century, Larsen argues that the freedom struggle began much earlier:

> [T]he freedom struggle in Goa was actually a process lasting nearly one hundred years by

---

[1] Priolkar, "Who is a Goan?" 269.
[2] Larsen, *Faces of Goa*, 43.
[3] *ibid.*, 45.

which (sic) few individuals first realised their subjugation and then diffused these ideas into the larger society in order to garner support. These ideas then became ideals, translated into institutions with the goal of realising the ideals of self rule, freedom and a democratic state."[4]

The Denationalisation of Goans, a pamphlet published in 1944 by the Goa Congress Committee (a part of the independence movement), was an effort to prove that Goa does not have any culture, to challenge the myths that Albuquerque was tolerant of Hindus and mixed marriages, and to argue that St. Francis Xavier did not convert many Goans to Christianity. According to the authors, these two men did not help to create a unique Goan identity, but created a region in India that does not have an identity.[5]

The pamphlet authors argued that because of the Portuguese, Goans did not obtain a European-Indian culture, but rather, no culture at all. The pamphlet is very anti-Portuguese and subjective; everything European, from the Portuguese language to the architecture, is criticised. Its main argument is that Goans should disregard the Portuguese aspect to their culture and accept an Indian identity. A Goan is:

> A servile follower of everything foreign in his country, hybrid in manners and habits, living in disharmony with his natural surroundings; his strange behavior makes one doubt the purity of his race, which nevertheless, in no way differs from that of the neighboring Indians.[6]

The major flaw in this argument is that if a Goan is a hybrid in manners and habits, then how can he be just like the neighboring Indians? Another statement made by the authors is that "the forced denationalisation of Goans is more

---

[4]Larsen, *op.cit.*, 50.
[5]Goa Congress Committee, *Denationalisation of Goans*, 59.
[6]*ibid*, 7.

marked because foreign rule has lasted longer in Goa than in other parts of India."[7]

It is true that parts of Goa were under foreign rule for four hundred and fifty years, but to say they have no identity because of Portuguese rule is a mere propaganda statement offered without proof. Goans have always identified themselves as Goan with distinct aspects of their culture reflecting a Portuguese part of their heritage.

Because culture and identity are not static, Goans are continuing to redefine themselves. Today, as Goa has more contact and trade with India, Goans are defining themselves more as Indians:

> [T]he cultural fusion and synergy which one would expect to find following a realignment and political identification with the Indian nation would result in a cultural drift towards becoming 'more Indian' and towards a greater identification with India rather than Portugal.[8]

The novel *Angela's Goan Identity*, reveals this shifting viewpoint. The author Carmo D'Souza discusses the problem of determining what is a Goan identity and its change over time.

A baby girl is born to a Christian Goan family and the problems of Goan identity surface when choosing their daughter's name. At the time of Angela's birth, Goa is still under Portuguese rule and Portuguese officials are attempting to quash feelings of nationalism. The local priest, in agreement with the Portuguese officials, insists that the new baby's name must be a Christian name.[9]

The family, however, has nationalist feelings and even though the priest insists that her name is Angela, the family calls her by an Indian version of that name, Anjali[10].

---
[7] Goa Congress Committee, *op.cit.*
[8] Larson, *op. cit.*, 51-52
[9] Carmo D'Souza, *Angela's Goan Identity*, 6
[10] *ibid*, 9

They believe that the child would benefit from going to a local school that teaches a local language, where she will learn about Indian culture rather than a school that teaches in Portuguese. Although the novel is silent on the issue, Angela's parents' desire to have her receive her education in Marathi indicates support for the Marathi side of the language debate over the use of Konkani, the traditional language of Goa.

The novel points out that it was rare for a Christian child to attend a Marathi school. Most Christian children in her village only took a few classes in Portuguese at the local primary school.[11] The conflict over the Marathi/Portuguese language issue is shown when some of Angela's relatives oppose her studying Marathi rather than Portuguese, because they fear it would be an obstacle in continuing her education.

Angela transfers schools when a new law requires Portuguese as the language of instruction in all primary schools. It is interesting to note that although Angela spends two years in the Marathi school, she learned very little about Indian culture because the educational emphasis fell on the script, reading and mathematics. She does learn, however, that Goans can speak and have a culture that is not Portuguese.

At the Marathi school, she asks her friend Atmaram if he is Goan and if he plays the violin, the piano, the guitar, or sings *fados* – the music genre then popular in Portuguese-ruled Goa which can be traced from the 1820s in Portugal, but probably has much earlier origins. He declares that playing instruments does not make a person Goan and fados are Portuguese songs. He replies that he sings patriotic songs instead.[12]

Atmaram serves to challenge Angela's concept of Goan

---

[11]Carmo D'Souza, *op. cit.*, 13.
[12]*ibid.*, 15.

identity. Angela thinks that her friend must be a Christian. She asks him: "But you are a Hindu? How can a Hindu be a true Goan?"[13] Calling her lack of knowledge of Goan history into question and revealing her ancestral roots, he answers, "Don't forget your forefathers were Hindus and they wore *dhotis*"[14] (the rectangular piece of unstitched cloth that is the traditional garment of men's wear in India).

Angela's changing concept of identity is revealed at the Portuguese school where young minds are instilled with a Portuguese identity and propaganda. At the Portuguese school, her name changes again to Anjinha because of the political overtones of the name Anjali. Angela quickly becomes mesmerized by a teacher at the new school and becomes indoctrinated with Portuguese concepts.[15]

The educational focus is so politically oriented that even children's drawings become political statements. The teacher instructs them to draw "gentlemen" as Europeans and not as Indians in native *dhotis*.[16]

The children study Portuguese literature, geography, and history and are taught catchy tunes to sing in praise of Portugal; they learn nothing about India or Indian culture. The students become convinced that Goa is part of Portugal, like Madeira and the Azores.[17] Even though Angela's family tells her that India is much bigger and more powerful than Portugal, she remains unconvinced and insists that her *professora* is correct.[18]

To show further the concept of a changing identity, Atmaram, Angela's childhood friend from her Marathi school, enrolls in the same Portuguese school and changes from a

---

[13] Carmo D'Souza, *op.cit.*, 17.
[14] *ibid.*, 18.
[15] *ibid.*, 19.
[16] *ibid.*, 21.
[17] *ibid.*, 24-25.
[18] *ibid.*, 28.

child who is very nationalist and proud of his Goan identity to believing that he is Portuguese in every way.

He becomes completely transformed by his Portuguese education and becomes militarily trained because he believes that he can help defend Goa when India invades it.[19] When India invades Portuguese-ruled Goa, and the latter falls with little resistance to the Indians, Atmaram does not adjust well: "Most of the students adapted to the change. There were a few who became victims in the process of the transition. Atmaram simply seemed unable to pick up the trend of the past to continue into the future."[20]

Dissatisfied and feeling out of place with his new school, he leaves Goa to finish his education in Portugal.[21] Angela, on the other hand, begins to see her identity as being Indian[22]. When she begins attending an English school, her name changes back again to Angela because it sounds more English.[23]

Again her identity and the language of her schooling are changed. After Angela graduates from school, she continues to maintain her "Indian identity" by marrying a man who is not Portuguese, Goan or Christian, but an Indian Sikh. Atmaram returns from Portugal for her wedding; he has maintained his "Portuguese identity" and culture by marrying a Portuguese woman from Coimbra.

Angela asks her friend, "Are you Portuguese now?"[24] Although Atmaram is a Portuguese citizen and has a "Portuguese identity", he cannot forget he is also Goan. He tells Angela, "I am Goan. As hundred percent as you are.... We never cease to be Goans."[25]

---

[19] Carmo D'Souza, *op. cit.*, 30-31.
[20] *ibid.*, 50.
[21] *ibid.*, 56.
[22] *ibid.*, 54.
[23] *ibid.*, 50.
[24] *ibid.*, 144.
[25] *ibid.*

In reality, he has assumed a dual Portuguese/Goan identity, and rejects the concept of an Indian identity even as Goa comes under Indian control. Angela points out that she knows Goans who have gone abroad, have become out of touch with Goan culture, acquired the identity of their new home, and still have a Goan identity. Atmaram admits: "Goan identity is progressively changing."[26]

Another novel that discusses the Portuguese educational system and how it influenced the formation of Goan identity is *Sorrowing Lies My Land*. Lambert Mascarenhas writes: "According to our books, Portugal was the world and the world, Portugal, and if there were any other places existing, they were not worth learning about."[27]

In the novel, Felipe (called Babu by his friends and family), makes the mistake of asking his teacher if Alfonso de Albuquerque spoke Konkani. The *professora* is annoyed by his question, but he persists in questioning her as to why Goans speak both Portuguese and Konkani. He cannot understand the complexity of Goan identity. He questions, if Goans are really Portuguese and not Indian, then why do they have a separate language?

> 'Did Alfonso de Albuquerque speak Konkani, *Professora*?' I asked that day.
>
> 'How silly of you, Felipe,' she exclaimed with a snigger. 'How could he? His language was Portuguese.'
>
> 'But we are Portuguese too, aren't we *Professora*? How's it then that our mother tongue is Konkani?'
>
> 'Who said that our mother tongue is Konkani? Ours is also Portuguese,' she explained.
>
> 'Ours also? Then what is Konkani?'

---

[26] *loc. cit.*
[27] Lambert Mascarenhas, *Sorrowing Lies My Land*, 35.

> The teacher was flustered and not wanting to proceed with this unpleasant subject said to me: 'Konkani is not a language. It is... it is... er... never mind what. Our language is Portuguese and we must speak it even in our homes. Do you understand?'[28]

The teacher's negative reaction to Konkani is explained by Frantz Fanon in *Black Skin White Masks*. Although Fanon speaks about colonialism and racism in Martinique, his criticisms about race, social class, and language also apply to Goa.

He notes that the official language in Martinique is French, and teachers watched their students closely to make sure they were not speaking in Creole. Fanon observes that in Brittany, France, there is a local dialect, but Bretons do not consider themselves to be inferior to other French people. In Martinique, however, speaking Creole implies that the person is less civilized and, therefore, inferior.[29] The Goan teacher's job is the same: to make sure that Goan students in Portuguese schools do not use the local language and that they learn that the Portuguese people are superior.

The novel *The Mango and the Tamarind Tree* by Leslie de Noronha gives an insight into the feelings of Goans who had a Portuguese identity that changed into a Goan one after the end of the colonial period.

On the surface, the novel deals with the affluent but disintegrating Albuquerque family. In reality, Noronha shows the disintegration of Portuguese identity in Goa by having the novel's main character Raoul break with many traditions. He refuses to go through an arranged marriage, falls in love with a woman from a lower class, and he sells the family home after his mother's death.

---

[28]Lambert Mascarenhas, op. cit.
[29]Fanon, *Black Skin White Masks*, 28.

Raoul's heritage is his enemy. It kept him from marrying the woman he loved and from the international career he loved. By giving up his traditions, Raoul symbolizes Goans giving up Portuguese traditions and shows the upheaval that frequently accompanies major political change and the reaction to it.

Raoul's family pressures him to settle down and to take care of the family estate just as his father had done; it is hard for them to accept changes. Raoul thinks about the pressure he is under:

> But even as he spoke, even though he was really in a temper, he knew the appointment had been made and he had to attend the party, no matter how furious he was with his aunt and mother, unless he was burning with fever, or dead. That was one of his enemies: tradition.[30]

Raoul's uncle Caesar explains how the end of colonialism is changing people's identities not only in Goa, but also all over the world. "Today countries are breaking through, demanding the right to achieve, actually achieving something worthwhile, establishing identities, homes, personalities, voices that are heard with grudging respect."[31]

While *Angela's Goan Identity* discusses different aspects of Goan identity, and the identity shifts that ordinary people underwent after Liberation, *The Mango and the Tamarind Tree* discusses the rejection of Portuguese colonial identity. Joseph K. Henry, a reviewer of *The Mango and the Tamarind Tree*, agrees that Noronha's intent is to show how the end of colonialism changed Goan identity:

> Noronha skillfully integrates the Goan historical past with contemporary time and issues of the day. The aftermath of colonialism not only provoked nostalgia but produced a staid aristocratic

---

[30] Noronha, *The Mango and the Tamarind Tree*, 63
[31] *ibid.*

class, a confused middle class and a disproportionate group of unskilled peasants.[32]

Henry also points out that the mango, Goa's national fruit, is symbolic in the novel of the uncorrupted colonial culture which is now only a memory. The fruit is a staple of the poor, yet it is also the foundation of Raoul's family wealth. The mango is "caught up in this web of contradictions and change...."[33] The people of Goa are likewise caught up in such a web and are seeking to find their own identity.

Maria, by K.A. Abbas, argues that Goans have an Indian identity. Maria is a Goan woman who fights against the Portuguese with six other Indian *satyagrahis* who are not only from different parts of India, but also from different castes and different religions. The mission of "The Seven Indians" is to sneak into Goa and hoist seven Indian flags at different strategic locations as a symbol of Indian support for the Goan revolutionaries. Because they belong to a non-violent protest group, they are not to use violence unless it is in self-defence.

The seven Indians have a hard time working together as a team at first because they have different backgrounds, but they learn to put aside their differences in order to help Maria for the benefit of the cause, and, because she is so young, they admire her courage. When she is given her Indian flag at the beginning of the mission, Maria begins to realize that she has an Indian identity that is distinct from her Goan identity:

> By now, each of them had taken out the flag that had become the symbol of Goa, and they were on the tenter hooks to find out whether she had accepted their gesture and their help. She looked from one face to the other, then she looked at

---

[32]Henry. "On Mango and Tamarind Tree," 13.
[33]*ibid.*, 13.

>   the flags. Then she wondered aloud, 'Seven flags and six Indians?'
>
>   Subodh replied, 'The seventh flag is for you.' And he handed the flag to her....
>
>   Tears of happiness welled into her eyes; for the first time on her face was the flicker of a smile as she said, with trembling lips, 'I am an Indian, too!'[34]

After that realization, Maria refers to herself as Indian. In the middle of the mission when the seven Indians are putting up an Indian flag, Anwar Ali confiscates a gun from a Portuguese official and refuses to give it to Maria. She wants to take the gun from him and bury it because she knows if the Portuguese catch them with it, they will be killed. Anwar Ali and Maria argue:

> 'Who are you to give me orders?'
> 'I am The Seventh Indian!'
> 'So what?' he answered, 'I am an Indian too!'
> 'I am the one who was born in Goa, whose father and uncles died in the struggle against the Portuguese, and my brother – the one whose clothes I am wearing – is still in their prison.' [35]

Maria's comment shows that although she has an Indian identity, she still has an additional belief that being Goan is slightly different from being Indian. She believes that she has a dual identity and is different from other Indians because of the struggle that she and her family have endured.

In contrast to the novel *Maria*, B.K. Boman-Behram in *Goa and Ourselves* argues that Goans have a Portuguese identity. The author is pro-Portuguese, and claims that the Portuguese were not racially prejudiced and that both Goans and the Portuguese had equal rights.[36]

---

[34] Abbas, *Maria*.
[35] *ibid.*, 81
[36] *ibid.*, 34

He states, "Look at any facet you like of Goan life and you will see Portugal deeply reflected in it. Ethnically and culturally, the Goans have been moulded to the Lusitanian type they remain by tradition and choice."[37] This author continues to praise the Portuguese by declaring that they respected local institutions, favored mixed marriages and attempted to assimilate native society to the social customs of Portugal.[38]

According to Boman-Behram, the Liberation movement, founded by Goans living in Bombay, grew only because of the support by the Indian government in New Delhi. He declares that in New Delhi the Liberation movement "has been nursed into the howling brat we see" and insists that Goans did not want their independence nor did they want to become part of India[39]. "No such desire has been expressed in any serious protest or internal risings by Goan nationals."[40]

At the time of Liberation and for some time thereafter, not all Goans had either a Portuguese or an Indian identity. Indeed, some were not supportive of Goa being part of either nation. Others believed that Goa traded Portuguese colonialism for Indian colonialism.

In *Homework*, by Suneeta Peres da Costa, the main character Mina is the daughter of Goans who migrated to Australia. Her father sees his identity as being neither Portuguese nor Indian but distinctly Goan. He made his children respond to the question, "Where are you from?" with the answer, "Goa."[41]

Mina states: "I was to explain that since Goa was illegally confiscated by the Indian state, my allegiance was technically not Indian but Portuguese."[42] Her father's belief that

---

[37]Boman-Behram, *Goa and Ourselves*, 57
[38]*ibid.*, 36-37
[39]*ibid.*, 22
[40]*ibid.*, 32
[41]Peres Da Costa, *Homework*, 156
[42]*ibid.*, 156

Goa should be independent from India was so strong that he compared the cause of Goa with that of other separatist groups such as the Sikhs, the Tamil Tigers, the Basques, and the Sinn Fein.[43]

In *Liberation: A Novel*, Jorge Ataide Lobo describes the conflicting definitions of Goan identity and how quickly Goans can change their identity. In his novel, Celina, a teacher in an English school, declares that she is not interested in joining the liberation movement against the Portuguese. She is offended and angry when Dinanath tells her she should support the movement because she is Indian:

> Indian! You offend me. I am Portuguese. I want Goa...our beautiful, peaceful Goa to continue Portuguese. You scum, you good-for-nothing idiots come here and incite the poor and ignorant. Do you think I am one of them? Do you think you can bribe me with your sweet talk? Get out...get out, I say, and leave me alone. [44]

Dinanath is determined not to leave her alone and states that her temper and passion will make her a good revolutionary. He asks her to keep an open mind and to think about joining them. After Celina cools off, she thinks about the liberation movement rationally, quickly has a change of heart and identity, and decides to join the revolutionaries.[45]

The author, however, also states that Goan identity is so distinct that it is truly neither Portuguese nor Indian but a mixture of the two. Lobo believes that Goans created a new consciousness from the values of the past with the new values of the present. This new consciousness is so distinctly Goan that it is, in reality, an Indian sub-nationality:

> Politically, we were Portuguese citizens, but we knew our territory was a colony. We could not

---
[43] Peres Da Costa, *op cit.*, 155
[44] Lobo, *Liberation: A Novel*, 107
[45] *ibid.*

call ourselves Indians, we did not feel we were really Portuguese. Then we created this consciousness of Goans. We were neither Indian nor Portuguese. We were Goans. We created for us a sort of sub-nationality.[46]

The view that Goans created this new attitude from the values of the past with the new values of the present to create a distinct Goan identity is a common theme in some Goan thought.

What seems like a contradiction is how Goans perceive their identity; the problem is that not only is change inevitable, but also that identity is defined differently by different people. Identity can change over time, and that identity itself can change within a person.

The autobiography of Telo de Mascarenhas, *When the Mango Trees Blossomed*, is a good example of changing identity. He began his life under the Portuguese colonial system, grew up in Goa and, like many Goans, had to go to Bombay or abroad to further his education. First he studied in Lisbon, went to law school in Coimbra, became a Public Prosecutor in Alentejo, a Magistrate of Public Faith in the Algarve, and married a Portuguese woman.[47]

His government position allowed him the time to read about India and Indian culture and he began to change his views on Goa.[48] He states:

> We Goans who had had our education in Goa were ignorant of everything which was ours. But we were taught the history of Portugal.... Once in Portugal, my school fellows and I read enthusiastically about India... which in Goa we were unable to do owing to the lack of texts, and be-

---

[46]Lobo, *op.cit.*, 222-23
[47]Mascarenhas, *Mango Trees Blossomed*, 68-80.
[48]*ibid.*, 80.

cause it was forbidden for us to do so for political reasons.⁴⁹

As Mascarenhas' political views changed in favour of Goa being independent from Portugal, so did his personal life. His marriage to the Portuguese woman ended in divorce, his eldest daughter died of pneumonia, and his younger daughter stayed in Lisbon and became a teacher. Mascarenhas reveals that he no longer had a Portuguese identity but an Indian one. He states:

> Eventually both of us realized that my own people had been right, and that wedlock with a foreigner was indeed 'nonsense'. We Indians are quite different from the people of other continents, both in temperament and in mental and spiritual outlook.... Indian women still preserve the virtues, though to a lesser extent now than in days gone by, of patience, a sense of duty and forbearance associated with the legendary figures of yore. Kunti, Sita, Draupadi, Savitri and so many others – qualities that are so necessary for the maintenance of peace and good understanding in family life.⁵⁰

Mascarenhas next decided to go to Goa by way of Bombay to start his pro-Goan political career by running *Ressurge, Goa!*, a Goan pro-independence newspaper.⁵¹

After India got its independence from England, he took long leave from his Portuguese government job rather than resigning, because he believed taking a leave of absence was politically less suspicious.⁵² His leave of absence, however, would come back to haunt him because the Portuguese government would use it against him. As soon as he returned to Goa, the authorities were looking for him:

---

⁴⁹Mascarenhas, *op.cit.*, 60.
⁵⁰*ibid.*, 83-84
⁵¹*ibid.*, 150
⁵²*ibid.*, 89

> The police in Goa, who had filed as criminal evidence with which to charge-sheet me, all the manuscripts, messages and poems I had sent to Bombay to the local newspapers, were alarmed at my presence in Goa, and let loose their hounds on my heels.[53]

When the police asked Mascarenhas to go to the police station, he refused, claiming that he was a Portuguese magistrate on leave and he would need permission from the Ministry to go to any police station or court.[54] Nevertheless, a warrant was issued for his arrest.

To avoid arrest he returned to Bombay where he continued his political writings and published anti-colonial leaflets.[55] Mascarenhas continued to voice his anti-Portuguese political views and made a radio speech stating that Goa would have maintained ties with Portugal if they could have an Indian identity:

> If Salazar had listened to our longings expressed in my message, and if afterwards he had not been so stubborn deliberately closing his eyes to realities, he would have averted much suffering and hardship from the poor Goans; Portugal could have maintained Goa in her language, her culture and her way of life; and Goans would have been happy living without resentment, maintaining their identity within India as Indians integrated in the mainstream of the country's life.[56]

In an attempt to stop Mascarenhas' political activities, the Portuguese government recalled him to resume his official position. He refused, got fired, became the editor of the na-

---

[53] Mascarenhas, *op. cit.*, 144
[54] *ibid.*, 145
[55] *ibid.*, 145-147
[56] *ibid.*, 153

tionalist paper *Ressurge, Goa!*, and married an Indian woman in New Delhi.[57]

Mascarenhas returned to Goa where he was arrested, deported to Lisbon and spent many years in jail as a political prisoner. Mascarenhas writes about his time in prison, "I was a notorious prisoner, not only because I was a Goan nationalist, but also because I had been awarded the highest maximum sentence by the political plenary court."[58]

Amnesty International, the Indian government, and the president of the International Red Cross tried to secure his release without success.[59] After President Salazar died, he was finally released from prison after serving ten years.[60] The author returned to Goa after it had become part of India.

Although race is not raised as an identity issue by other Goan authors, Margaret Mascarenhas' *Skin* focuses on a different aspect of Goan identity. Unlike other novels about Goans, Mascarenhas' novel is one of the few that reveals that race is an aspect of Goan identity.

The main character of her novel, Pagan, is originally Goan; but she was reared in the United States. When she visits her grandmother in Goa, she discovers not only her heritage, but also the skeletons in her family tree. She is not the biological daughter of her parents, she is the fair-skinned biracial product of her uncle's relationship with a servant of African descent.

At first, she is confused when she believes that her grandmother does not recognize her. Her aunt reproves Pagan for her appearance: "She recognized you. She just didn't want to acknowledge your skin. It is because you are tanned like a coconut from your travels under the Angolan sun."[61] Pagan does not understand why her skin colour matters to

---
[57] Mascarenhas, *op.cit*, 144-147
[58] *ibid.*, 230
[59] *ibid.*, 245
[60] *ibid.*, 253
[61] Margaret Mascarenhas, *Skin*, 34

her grandmother until she discovers that she is of mixed heritage.

Pagan's grandmother states that even though she did not have much for a dowry, she was able to marry a wealthy man because of her fair skin.[62]

The grandmother does not understand why Pagan does not appreciate her fair skin and her Goan heritage and use it to her advantage:

> Because of my efforts, as well as my superior genes, Maria (Pagan's Christian name) is perceived as a legitimate White woman in the white world; and as an aristocrat in Goa. Still she would defy me.... Baking herself in the sun like a raisin. Stupid girl. Why should I recognize her?[63]

The grandmother's comments indicate that she believes that being fair-skinned is an essential part of being part of the Goan upper class. She neither recognizes Pagan's other heritage, nor does she acknowledge her upbringing in the United States. What is important to the grandmother is that she sees Pagan as Goan, therefore Pagan should act Goan, and in this case, Goan is defined as being upper class, with fair skin and of Portuguese descent.

The grandmother's view reflects certain fundamental aspects of the social system that remained unchanged: views about race and social status. She is incapable of admitting the other half of Pagan's genetic inheritance and the low social status of the other grandmother.

While most Goan literature that discusses Goan identity focuses on the time period before Goa became part of India or during the Liberation struggle, *The Greater Tragedy*, a play by Lambert Mascarenhas, discusses Goan identity after Goa became part of India.

---

[62]Margaret Mascarenhas, *op.cit.*, 195-96
[63]*ibid.*, 196

The character Artimizia declares that Goa should have become independent and that Goans are losing their unique identity:[64] "I do not deny that bridges, hotels, industries have been established in Goa after Liberation, but we have lost our peace and the Goan people their Goanness."[65]

She further claims that she was happier during the Portuguese dictatorial rule than she is in a post-Liberation Indian democracy.[66]

Anil, another character, agrees with Atimizia that Goans have changed after Liberation, "but you must know the fact that the entire fabric of Goan society has become rotten and thus decaying since Liberation."[67] He says to his grandfather, Manuel Antonio, that corruption has become a way of life in Goa now and that it is a post-Liberation import from India.[68]

IDENTITY does not remain static, but instead it constantly undergoes changes; even among generations, there are differences between attitudes and opinions. Goa became part of India over 40 years ago, but there are still Goans who view themselves as "Portuguese."

Most Goans, however, view themselves as being Goan or Indian, or both. While identifying with the Portuguese and having Portuguese citizenship was a debated issue before and during Liberation, most Goans today do not believe they are Portuguese. There are Goans, however, who continue to speak Portuguese and still love some aspects of Portuguese culture, but they do not claim to have a Portuguese identity.

---

[64] Lambert Mascarenhas, *The Greater Tragedy*, 13
[65] *ibid.*, 11
[66] *ibid.*, 10
[67] *ibid.*, 80
[68] *ibid.*, 4

Victor Rangel-Ribeiro, a Goan writer, explains that their identity is similar to those who are French speakers in Louisiana. They have a distinct culture, and maintain their linguistic ties, but regard themselves as being definitely Americans.

Many Goans view themselves the same way. They have a distinct culture, but they are Indians.[69] Others view Goan identity as being similar to that of Puerto Ricans, who have a Puerto Rican identity but see no contradiction in being American.

While the borders of Goa have long been established, Goan identity will continue to be complex and controversial. As more time goes by, however, Portuguese influence will continue to decrease. Fewer Goans are learning Portuguese, although it is now being taught at Goa University at Taleigao, outside Panjim.

More migrants are moving into Goa from other parts of India, and more Goans are leaving to work and be educated abroad. Because of the huge changes Goa is now undergoing, the issue of who is a Goan, and what constitutes Goan identity, will continue to change.

---

[69]Victor Rangel-Ribeiro. Personal interview.

Chapter 4

Choosing a tongue

THE LANGUAGE debate in Goa is ongoing, with the supporters of Konkani and Marathi continuing their arguments for the language favoured, although the issue was supposed to have been settled in 1987. Within Konkani, there is also the issue over script. The choice of an official state language indicated the choice of an identity in Goa,[1] but the belief that having an official language establishes a separate identity is a concept that began in the nineteenth century.

Benedict Anderson states that until the nineteenth century, political boundaries in Europe almost never coincided with language communities. Most literate Europeans communicated in different languages and no one believed that those languages belonged to any defined group.[2] As more people became conscious of defining themselves in terms of their nationality, language became an important issue in many nationalist movements, including Goa.[3]

In order to achieve statehood, Goa had to decide which of the two native languages, Marathi or Konkani, would be

---
[1]Childs and Williams, *Introduction to Post-Colonial Theory*, 193
[2]Anderson, *Imagined Communities*, 196
[3]*ibid.*, 196-97

the official one. The majority of voters had decided in the Opinion Poll of 1967 that Goa would maintain a separate and independent identity, and not merge into neighbouring Maharashtra, a state formed with Marathi as its official language. This vote, however, did not conclusively settle the issue of language. In 1987, after a bitter linguistic dispute that spanned two years, Konkani became Goa's official language and it was also recognized as one of the national languages of India in the Eighth Schedule of the Constitution in 1992.

Some Goans believe that Portuguese should be eradicated in Goa because it is used only by the upper class and it is not a useful language to learn here currently. In reality, the number of Portuguese speakers in Goa is declining and the language debate today is really between Marathi and Konkani.

While Marathi has been taught for many years in Goan schools, it is identified as part of a Maharashtrian identity. Because politicians used the Marathi issue to argue that Goa should be part of Maharashtra, many Goans fear they will lose their Goan identity if Marathi becomes the official language. As Robert S. Newman points out, choosing Konkani as the official language marked official recognition of Goan identity.[4]

The language debate continues. At times it has been so heated that protests have erupted into violence. Opinions about this issue can be found in all manner of writings: novels, periodicals, essays, editorial sections of newspapers, and on the Internet. Most of the opinions visible in this sphere support the position that Konkani and not Marathi should be the official language and that Konkani is an essential part of their identity.

However, linguistically, Goans are not unified.

Luis Santa Rita Vas divides the people into three linguistic groups. The first consists of those who have had a Por-

---

[4]Newman, "Konkani Mai Ascends the Throne," 55

tuguese identity and speak both Portuguese and Konkani. These people are called *assimilados* ("the assimilated"). During Portuguese rule, there was no dispute that Portuguese was the official language; today Portuguese in Goa is a dying language although it is taught as a foreign language at Goa University.

The second group reacted violently to foreign rule, resisted the Portuguese cultural and religious onslight, and remained fervent Hindus and spoke [or supported] mostly Marathi. They had a deeply-rooted kinship with neighbourng India, which they cultivated zealously, explains Vas. The third section – comprising mainly, but not exclusively, the poorer people – let foreign customs seep into and mingle with their lives. From this emerged a new culture, with their music, folk tales, proverbs, cooking and architecture acquiring a "widely-recognised distinctiveness".

The fourth group of Goans are those who migrated across the globe "finding Goa too small to fulfil their ambitions".[5]

Language is such an important issue in Goa because "it is not merely a creative device, but it also has implications for cultural identity."[6] This conflict was not really a serious problem until after Liberation, when Portuguese was no longer an official language. Goans became divided and many supporters of Konkani and Marathi wrote propaganda in support of one language or the other. The Marathi versus Konkani debate became such a political hot potato that it is still being fiercely debated today.

WHILE a native language is an essential part of Goan identity, some Goans advocate that it is more important to learn English in order to communicate and conduct

---
[5] Vas, *Modern Goan Short Stories*, viii.
[6] Arthur Rubinoff, *Political Community*, 116

business in the world. Indeed, English is widely studied and spoken in Goa.

The language issue, however, has broad implications. The majority of Christians and Hindus in South Goa favor Konkani while the Hindus in North Goa near Maharashtra favor Marathi. In addition to being an identity issue, it also seems to be a political control issue. Rubinoff points out that before Goa became a state, Prime Minister Rajiv Gandhi stated that Goa lacked the maturity for statehood and that the language issue had to be resolved before statehood would be granted.[7]

After Goa became part of India, it first became a territory rather than a state, but many Goans believed that territorial status was the same as second class citizenship. This belief has merit because union territories in India are totally controlled financially by New Delhi. In addition, the government in New Delhi could intervene or delay legislation, and it controlled the judicial system.

Because the federal government was slow to respond to the problems in Goa, many Goan politicians pushed for statehood. Other politicians advocated a merger with the state of Maharashtra. Advocates for statehood believed it would advance the development of Konkani, but "[a]s Konkani has five different scripts, a separate state with a single language would not necessarily have promoted the language's development."[8] A secondary problem arose in the use of English in administration and as a neutral language to avoid having to choose between Konkani and Marathi.[9]

In the later half of the nineteenth century, Christian migrants to Bombay and Pune established a journal, and religious and other works were written in the Roman script. The language of worship in the Christian community con-

---

[7]Arthur Rubinoff, *op cit.*, 118
[8]*ibid.*, 117
[9]*ibid.*, 117

tinued to be Konkani.[10] The First Provincial Congress in 1916 approved elementary education in Konkani. The first government schools in Konkani, however, were opened after Liberation in 1962, but the local parish schools taught Konkani.

Prabhakar S. Angle examines the history of the education system in Goa and states that formal Marathi education began in Mapusa in 1890 and other Marathi schools opened quickly after the first one. The Portuguese then opened bilingual "Luso-Marathi" (Portuguese-Marathi) schools, but they were not successful.

Angle declares that the Marathi schools were important because they were private and paid for by Hindus in order to educate their children in their "mother tongue."[11] The author states that, "for a long time Hindus have been imparting primary education to their children in Marathi."[12] "Christians, barring a few exceptions, did not learn Konkani either; instead, they sent their children to Portuguese or English-medium schools."[13]

The author writes that Christians had the advantage of parish schools run by Church authorities, but Hindus did not have access to these schools so they supported Marathi schools instead. He insists that it wasn't until the 1930s that some people came to believe that Konkani was a separate language, and not a dialect of Marathi.

Supporters of Konkani began to claim that Konkani was the mother tongue of all Goans.[14] It is interesting that Angle declares that an education in Marathi is a custom that only Hindus follow. He presents nothing in support of this statement, and the language debate as reflected in the novels set in the 1940s and 1950s does not support such a statement.

---

[10] Couto, "Foreword", xvi-xvii.
[11] Angle, *Goa Concepts and Misconcepts*, 69
[12] *ibid.*
[13] Santa Rita Vas, "Introduction", viii.
[14] Angle, *ibid.*, 69

In *Angela's Goan Identity*,[15] the child's Christian parents are criticized for sending their child to a Marathi elementary school. The changes in Angela's identity and the concomitant political changes in Goa are shown by the different languages in which she is educated, her relationship with other people, and how the language they use defines their identity.

Margaret Drucker's novel *Mangoes and Chappaties*, set during the period of British Rule in India, satirises a family's struggle to handle the language controversy. When the family is residing in Goa, Constancio's mother initiates a conversation from the previous day and asks: "What use is Portuguese. Who's going to Portugal?" The father takes over and adds: "It's true; few Goans know Portuguese. We use Konkani everywhere, with Hindu Goan, Catholic Goan, and Muslim Goan. We need Portuguese only for Salazar [the Portuguese ruler]".[16] His wife then replies that it is better to know English rather than Portuguese or Konkani when living in India. Constancio, the son, has aspirations to move up the social ladder and relocates to Bangalore for better opportunities. He is disgusted that a cousin, who speaks fluent English, does not use his language skills to his advantage:

> Constancio was consumed and irritated that Reuther could be so satisfied, without portfolio, degree, money, recognition, titles – no nothing. And strangely, no disgrace. With his knowledge and confidence he could be a college professor instead of providing free English classes in a beat-up reading room.[17]

Constancio resolves that his family will learn English. Drucker further satirizes the language controversy by having Constancio make up a complicated set of rules; his wife

---
[15]Carmo D'Souza, *Angela's Goan Identity*, 13
[16]Drucker, *Mangoes and Chappaties*, 17
[17]*ibid.*, 64

can only speak English to their daughter, but if she is speaking to another person in the daughter's presence, she has to speak Konkani, and finally she has to speak only English with him. He believes his children will learn Konkani if they hear their mother speaking it with other people.[18] His hilarious set of complicated rules emphasize the importance of learning English and fitting into British India.

While the Goa Legislative Assembly passed the Official Languages Act (Act No. 5 of 1987) which made Konkani in the Devanagari script the official language, it also provided for the use of Marathi in Goa and Gujarati in Daman and Diu. In reality, "[n]o political party got what it wanted, as the Goa Congress had fought for Konkani with Roman script and the MGP or Maharashtrawadi Gomantak Party championed Marathi. In reality the issue was moot, as English was entrenched as the language of both education and administration."[19]

Earlier, the merger controversy (over whether Goa should merge into Maharashtra or stay separate, an issue which would have linguistic overtones) was decided in an historic Opinion Poll held on January 16, 1967:

> [The Opinion Poll] [w]as itself unique and the only one of its kind in the history of independent India. Other states in the country like Maharashtra and Andhra Pradesh and more recently, Jharkhand and Uttaranchal, got recognition of their unique and distinct identity by agitational methods.... Andhra Pradesh was delinked from the Madras Presidency after a long and bitter struggle. It was only in Goa that conflicting demands on whether Goa should retain its unique and distinct identity or should be merged with

---

[18] Drucker, *op. cit.*, 73
[19] Arthur Rubinoff, *op. cit.*

Maharashtra was decided democratically.[20] Konkani supporters won the Opinion Poll, but it was a very narrow margin of only around 30,000 votes. If the Marathi supporters had won, Goa would have become a district or a *taluka* (sub-district) of Maharashtra. According to editor Rajan Narayan, "[t]he unique and distinct identity of Goa would have been forever destroyed. Indeed, there would have been no Goa except for the valiant fight put up by secular minded Goans cutting across linguistic and ethnic barriers."[21]

An examination of other forms of Goan literature written between 1944 and the present reflects a language debate that is ongoing.

In 1944, an anti-Portuguese pamphlet, *The Denationalization of Goans*, published by the Goa Congress Committee, argued that Goans were not interested in the Marathi-Konkani language debate because the educated class abhors using local languages and prefers Portuguese.[22]

Overlooking the fact that the bureaucracy used Portuguese, the group argues that Portuguese was not a very useful language to learn. At the time this document was written, it was not used for business. The authors also point out the deficiencies of a Portuguese education. At that time there were no scientific or technological texts in Portuguese, but instead French texts were used in the classroom.[23]

A.K. Priolkar's *Goa: Facts versus Fiction*, published in 1962, is a pro-Marathi argument wherein the author claims that Goan identity is a really Maharashtrian one, and Goa should become part of the state of Maharashtra. The author argues that Goa does not have a separate identity:

> In the 'New Conquests'... the impact of Portuguese culture has been superficial and slight....

---

[20] Narayan, "Essence of Goan Identity,"
[21] *ibid.*
[22] Goa Congress Committee, *Denationalization of Goans*, 45
[23] *ibid.*, 47

> It is a mistake, therefore to consider the present Goa as a homogeneous area having a distinctive cultural identity.[24]

There are two flaws in Priolkar's arguments. He does not take into account the Old Conquests which were greatly impacted by Portuguese rule, and he uses only the New Conquest areas to make the assumption that all of the areas of Goa have the same Marathi identity. *Goa: Facts versus Fiction* does not offer any comparisons or data on other areas of India to support the claim that Goan culture is a Marathi one.

On the Marathi side of the argument, the author states that Konkani is an old dialect of Marathi. He points out that Jesuits called it the "Lingua Bramana" or high Marathi. The term Konkanis also refers to the Hindus in Goa, as well as people from the Konkan region. Konkani also varies with each locality as well as between castes.

The author argues that there is no remaining pre-Portuguese literature in Konkani, not because it didn't survive, but because none existed. It was all in Marathi. He states, "There is lots evidence of a positive character to show that Marathi has always been the only literary language of Goa."[25] Priolkar also argues that Marathi, not Konkani, should be the official language because the use of local dialects will divide the state; what is needed is a standard language.

Although Hindi is an official national language, it is only used in part of India. The author is convinced that scholars who are against Marathi are against the language because they suffered from discrimination when they left Goa to live in Bombay.[26] This is a very weak argument because he quotes no statistics, oral histories, or other data to sub-

---

[24] Priolkar, *Goa: Fact versus Fiction*, 8
[25] *ibid.*, 23
[26] *ibid.*, 12

stantiate this claim. Proving a discrimination claim would be difficult because he offers no supporting data to show that it caused them to oppose Marathi as the state language of Goa.

One point that the author does make is that if Konkani became the official state language it could be a problem because it is written in at least four different scripts: Devanagari, Kannada, Malayalam, and Roman: "[i]f Konkani is selected, they will have to face a host of problems, such as the choice of the form of Konkani to be used in schools, choice of script, etc... any change should be implemented gradually to allow time for the views of the Christian community to crystallise (sic)... [and to] avoid taking any decisions which would prejudice the issue."[27] Priolkar's view seems to be a reasonable approach, but it does not take into consideration the fact that the majority of Goans prefer Konkani rather than Marathi.

In the introduction to *Ferry Crossing: Short Stories from Goa*, Manohar Shetty explains the reason Marathi became a popular language in Goa:

> While Konkani was laid low for centuries by the Inquisition, Marathi was kept alive as the language of the princely courts. It was also the language in which the Hindu scriptures were preserved during the height of Portuguese religious repression.[28]

Shetty continues to explain that by the time of the Portuguese takeover of the northern parts of Goa, near the state of Maharashtra, the Portuguese position on learning local languages had softened. Marathi thrived in the northern part of Goa, and the Goan administration used it as an official language. Shetty also states that the battle between Marathi and Konkani divided Goa and, until recently, pre-

---

[27]Priolkar, *op. cit.*, 46
[28]Shetty, "Introduction", xv.

vented the production of high quality literature. He believes, "[t]he responsibility of creating a tradition, at least in the area of fiction, rests on the current crop of writers."[29]

In *My Goa: An Autobiography*, Luizinho Faleiro, a Goan politician, reveals himself to be a staunch supporter of Konkani. In 1982, he drafted a resolution to not only make Konkani the state language, but also to develop a Konkani academy. Faleiro describes his two main political goals in Goa were the promotion of Konkani and Goan statehood. To obtain more support for Konkani, he states, "I interacted with Konkani lovers, writers, thinkers, playwrights."[30]

The Konkani movement was a way in which Goa could oust the Maharashtrawadi Gomantak Party, also called the MGP, which was pro-Marathi, and wanted to merge Goa with Maharashtra during the 1960s. Faleiro asks: "Who... would redeem Goa from the disastrous effects of the well-intentioned but hopelessly misdirected and tragically executed MGP policies between 1963 and 1979?"[31] Faleiro describes the chaotic situation that some Konkani supporters faced:

> Eventually but finally under pressure, Chief Minister Rane, who was not really a Konkani apostle, accepted our logic. All of the other ministers were equally luke-warm. It was only when people virtually attacked them that they ran to New Delhi and said, "No, we can't go back to Goa without an assurance on Konkani." They had been physically attacked by the people. Francisco Sardinha's house had been ransacked. Pronto Barbosa's house had been ransacked...[32]

---

[29] Shetty, *op. cit.*, xvi.
[30] Faleiro, *My Goa*, 56
[31] *ibid.*, 54
[32] *ibid.*, 95

64 CHAPTER 4. CHOOSING A TONGUE

Robert S. Newman points out that an early move to merge Goa with Maharashtra was defeated in 1967. The MGP, however, remained in power until 1979. But at the end of its power, it was perceived by the people as being corrupt, dominated by one person, and in favour of only lower caste Hindus.[33]

Despite what earlier writers such as A.K. Priolkar contend, Marathi has not always been more popular than Konkani. Since Liberation, Konkani has become more popular. Sharmila Kamat declares: "Everyone is speaking Konkani nowadays."[34] *Mango Mood*, a collection of "tongue-in-cheek" essays by Kamat, published in 1995, were originally written as contributions to newspapers and magazines, about different aspects of Goan society. She discusses the problems of establishing an official language in the essay "Tongue of Violence" (written about 1990), and states that the language issue in Goa and the attendant problems resulted from the increased popularity in learning Konkani. "Konkani has progressed from being not merely a tongue for discussion but the tongue under discussion."[35]

Kamat argues that the new popularity of Konkani has caused new political agitations and violent protests by parents. As a result of the violence, the author argues, young students are learning that violence is the language of choice. She sarcastically declares that violence is a language that does not have a difficult time finding instructors; it is one language that has widespread support from all aspects of Goan society.[36]

Another Konkani supporter, Nora Secco de Sousa, states that there is no longer a controversy between Konkani and Marathi. According to her, "If the Sahitya Akademi, a supreme senate of experts of Indian literature, has recog-

---

[33] Newman, "Goa: Transformation." 22
[34] Kamat "Tongue of Violence," 34.
[35] *ibid.*
[36] *ibid.*, 35

nized Konkani as an independent language than (sic) the controversy about it being a dialect of Marathi or a full-fledged language no longer exists."[37] The author declares that Konkani is one of India's oldest Indo-Aryan languages and was one of the first to publish a modern grammar. According to her, Konkani needed to be made the State's official langauge:

> Thus it is imperative that it should be... made the official language of Goa.... It is only in this way that Goan interests can be protected, the sons of the soil assured of employment opportunities, and the homeland be saved. This is an S.O.S. so Goans awaken, and show that you are not all that *susegad* as you seem.[38]

Ironically, after the 1967 defeat of the proposed merger between Goa and Maharashtra, the MGP made a complete about-face. They declared their support for statehood, a separate Goan university, and the recognition of Konkani as one of the constitutionally recognized national languages.[39] Despite this, as has been noted, the issue of whether Marathi or Konkani should be the official language is still a hotly contested issue.

In June 2000, the periodical *Goa Today* published the opinions of ten Goans on whether Goa should become a bilingual state and give Marathi equal status as Konkani. Of the ten people interviewed, eight of them believe that Marathi should not be an official state language in Goa. The one person who believed that Marathi should be an official language stated that he believed Konkani and Marathi enjoyed equal status under the Official Language Act, but that was not the case after the court ruled otherwise.

Gopalrao Mayekar declared, "For centuries ... the Marathi language had a predominating position in multifar-

---

[37] De Souza, "Konknni My Mother Tongue," 71.
[38] *ibid*.
[39] Newman, "Goa: Transformation." 22.

ious aspects of Goan life."[40] Pointing out that there is a rich history of Marathi literature and that Marathi was the language of instruction for many years, he stated that Marathi is so important to Goan Hindus that they have always used Marathi for rituals and self expression.[41] Mayekar further argued that Marathi is a crucial part of Goan history, "[e]ven the freedom movement and social reforms had taken inspiration from [the] Marathi language."[42]

Manohar Hirba Sardessai, another Marathi supporter, believed both languages are part of the heritage of Goans, therefore both languages should be cherished by giving them equal status as official state languages.[43] He also felt that Marathi should have equal status because it has a strong relationship with Konkani. He says: "I feel that Konkani is nothing but undeveloped Marathi language."[44]

Sardessai argues that the Portuguese conquistadors used Marathi because Father Thomas Stephens (1549-1619) wanted to use a unified language when he wrote *The Life of Jesus*, so that people in different regions of the state could read it.[45] Marathi did not have several dialects, but Konkani had two, a coastal dialect, Canarim, and the more developed Brahmanic Canarim.[46]

On the other side of the language debate, Konkani supporters argue that Konkani should be the official language of Goa because it is spoken by ninety five percent of Goans. Sudha Amonkar, an educator, declares that, "Goa is a small state and 95 per cent of the people speak Konkani, dream Konkani and think Konkani. Although some people say that they speak Marathi, their thinking will definitely be in

---

[40]Vinayak Naik, "Marathi? No way!", 36.
[41]*ibid.*
[42]*ibid.*
[43]*ibid.*, 37.
[44]*ibid.*
[45]*ibid.*
[46]*ibid.*

Konkani."[47]

She feels that this issue was decided a long time ago and that it is an issue today only because certain politicians use this issue for their own agenda. She is adamant that Goa should only have one state language because, "[a]ll other States in India have only one official language and so should Goa."[48]

Another Konkani supporter also points out that even though the language issue was settled in the 1980s, Marathi continues to be used for all official purposes. Naguesh Karmali states that under the Language Act, Marathi is permitted for all official purposes and N. Shivdas challenges Marathi supporters to provide proof of where its use is prohibited.

He says, "In fact all press notes, literature of publicity, official invitations issued by the Information Department are in English and Marathi, and not in Konkani."[49] He declares that the argument "that if Marathi is not given equal status as Konkani, it will be removed from educational, literary fields is pure nonsense.[50]" Naik finds the argument to be flawed because the Portuguese permitted Marathi to be used.[51]

According to N. Shivdas, Marathi should not get much support because its supporters have changed their stand repeatedly on the language issue. At first they claimed that Konkani was a dialect of Marathi, and after they were unable to get Goa to merge with Maharashtra, they declared that Konkani was a separate language.[52]

Shivdas hopes that "in the end they will realise that they are in fact Konkani speaking people and [that] Konkani is

---

[47] Naik, *op. cit.*
[48] *ibid.*
[49] *ibid.*
[50] *ibid.*
[51] *ibid.*
[52] *ibid.*, 37-38.

their language."[53] M. Boyer points out that Konkani really is the language of Marathi speakers in Goa because, "[t]he hilarious irony is that these Marathi protagonists speak in Konkani while demanding equal status for Marathi."[54]

The controversy over which language should be the official one of Goa and which should be taught in primary schools does not seem to be dwindling. In 2003, in the Cyber Voices section of the *Navhind Times on the Web*, several Goans have expressed their strong opinions either for Konkani or for Marathi.

Niraj George, a Konkani supporter, writes the catchy slogan, "Goa for Konkani!! Konkani for Goa!!"[55] He firmly believes that Konkani can be the only language for Goa because, "[t]he spoken language of the state is the official language of the state." He also states that Marathi is a dialect of Konkani (rather than the other way around) and that Marathi supporters should go to Maharashtra because it is a non-Goan language.[56]

William 'Fire' Apechu believes that the only reason the Marathi/Konkani debate continues is because of "misguided, power-hungry language chauvinists." He criticizes politicians who send their own children to elite English schools, yet they "cry loud and clear about the 'merits' of providing education in some unimportant language.[57]" Apechu continues with his criticism by stating that learning a local language will create a mass of Goans who are unemployable and have a state that will be unable to conduct business with the rest of the world.[58] "Goa would do well to ignore such languages that have died a long time ago as far as the written word is concerned... and concentrate on

---

[53] Naik, *op. cit.*
[54] *ibid.*
[55] *ibid.*
[56] *ibid.*
[57] *ibid.*
[58] *ibid.*

our present language English and do as best as we can with it."[59]

Ravikant Anand Bhat believes that neither Konkani nor Marathi should be criticized, but he disagrees that English should be the medium of instruction instead of local languages. While learning English is essential in order to conduct business, the problem with English is that it is a foreign language and it brings with it a foreign culture.[60] Konkani is not a dead language because more people are conducting research on it. Konkani grammars are being written and literary works are being translated from Hindi into Konkani.[61]

Another writer, Romeo Raposo, believes that politicians are using the language debate as a way to continue the fight for a merger with Maharashtra. He declares, "They [Marathi supporters] wanted to merge Goa with Maharashtra and when it proved futile, they are now trying to saddle the language from another state to ours."[62]

Nikhil Burde agrees that politicians are deliberately keeping the issue alive: "It is easy for the politicians to make such statement to gather support from [a] gullible public by fanning their emotions."[63] Burde offers a solution on how to eliminate the language issue from being used by politicians: let the people of Goa decide in which language they want their children educated.[64]

While the Marathi-Konkani debate continues in Goa, it is not an identity issue for those who have emigrated.

Karin Larsen states that, "Among migrated Goans, their mother tongue Konkani has fallen out of use amongst the younger generation, especially in an urban environment like Bangalore where English is the language of employment."

---

[59] *Naik, op. cit.*
[60] *ibid.*
[61] *ibid.*
[62] *ibid.*
[63] *ibid.*
[64] *ibid.*

The trend towards using English instead of Konkani has affected the spread and growth of Konkani. For example, a Konkani theatre group in Bangalore did not fare well before a Goan audience because people there did not understand Konkani well enough to understand the humour.[65] Goan authors who live outside of Goa and write in English include Lino Leitao, Victor Rangel-Ribeiro, Ben Antao, and Peter Nazareth.

Although many Goans are learning English, most of them believe that learning a native language is crucial to maintaining their culture and unique identity. The language issue has been a controversial topic for about fifty years, but it is resurrected periodically.

There are many people who feel that preserving the native language of their particular heritage, be it Christian or Hindu, is an important aspect of preserving their Goan identity. As many Goans live abroad for a period of time and then either return or stay in their adopted country, they do not seem to be as concerned about the language issue.

Many have adopted a third identity – be it Canadian, Australian, American, or that of another country – and realise that their children do not have the same emotional ties to Goa, and do not identify themselves by language. Many Goans who remain in Goa believe that there should not be a language debate because learning English is more important. It is studied in school, widely spoken, and used in business, especially in the lucrative tourist industry.

Some have become cynical and feel that the language issue has been resolved and it is the politicians who keep the controversy alive to serve their own political goals. Nevertheless, many Goans feel that their native language, be it Marathi or Konkani, it an important part of what makes a Goan a Goan.

---

[65]Larsen, *Faces of Goa*, 378

Chapter 5

Expats, and home

The Village Home

WHEN GOA was conquered by the Portuguese in 1510, they made it the center of their maritime empire which stretched from the east coast of Africa to Malacca, and it became a major Christian center. The population was about 60,000 in the 1580s and by 1600 the population stood at approximately 75,000.[1]

In the seventeenth century, Portugal's fortunes began to decline, ships could no longer dock at the city of Goa because of the silting problem in the Mandovi River, and disease reduced the population until it stood at 20,000 by 1700. In 1751, the viceroy moved to Pangim (present day Panaji) and the population followed the viceroy.

In 1843, Panjim became the capital of Goa. While present-day Velha Goa (Old Goa) is a historic site, Panaji or Panjim has become Goa's third-largest city after Vasco and Margao, with a population of 65,000 (a metropolitan population of 100,000 if suburbs are included).

It has been estimated that approximately forty-one percent of the population of Goa's 1.2 population live in urban

---

[1] M.N. Pearson, *The Indian Ocean*, 155.

areas as there has been a large migration to the cities and towns.² (At the time of publishing, the estimated population was nearly 1.4 million, of which the urban population was about half.)

Since Liberation, the urban population has experienced a fourfold increase. Not all the urban growth has been caused by migrating Goans and by natural population increase; there has been an influx of migrants from other parts of India. In addition to industrial growth and tourism, the mining industry continues to play a large role in Goa's economy and is largely responsible for reducing the exodus of job seekers to the urban areas.³

In spite of the increase in industry, Goa has always been largely comprised of small agriculture-based communities. According to John Correia Afonso:

> Next to language, the most distinctive feature of Goan society is the millennial institution of the *gauponn* or communidade. This village community is a peculiar and characteristic organization which has existed from the earliest times in Goa.⁴

While Goa's rulers may have changed from time to time, "the attachment and fidelity of Goans to their village is greater than their loyalty to the rulers."⁵

John Correia Afonso notes that the institution of *gauponn* was not abolished under the Portuguese as it was in India under the British. He feels that it is useful today as it embodies a tradition of equality and social justice. It has developed in the Goan a deep-rooted love for his village. It also serves as the basis for his activities: political, economic, social, educational and cultural.⁶

---

²Angle, *An Economic Update*, 23.
³*ibid.*, 80.
⁴Correia Afonso, "To Cherish and to Share," 5.
⁵SarDessai, *History of Konkani Literature*, 7
⁶Correia Afonso, *ibid.*, 5.

The family, especially one's ancestors, and the ancestral home are also an important part of Goan identity which has been explored extensively in Goan literature which explores the yearning to return to the village and the ancestral home.

While the return from exile is a recurrent theme in literature, a concurrent important theme is the importance of the ancestral home and the village. A family home that can be passed on to future generations in the family is the most prized possession a Goan can have.

The short story *Back to the Village* by J.P. D'Souza emphasizes the importance of returning to the ancestral home and the resulting problems for the younger generation who do not share the same emotional ties to the village as their father. The main character, Jacob D' Costa, decides to retire early and leave Bombay after he is mugged on his way to work.

Although he tells his wife he wishes to return to Goa because of the increase in crime in Bombay, in reality he wants to return because of nostalgia: "Besides as one who was born in Goa, he looked with nostalgia to his ancestral land, as did most of his people. In this frame of mind he had decided to go back and settle in Goa."[7]

Jacob's wife, also Goan, understands that Goan "roots reached deep down,"[8] but she is not happy that her husband wants to uproot the family to move back home. Expressing a common concern, she has reservations about disrupting their children's education.

Goa's educational system was deficient at that time. The date of the setting of this story cannot be determined, but it must be prior to the establishment of Goa University in 1985. The oldest son, like many Goans, must leave Goa to pursue an education in engineering. The daughter, Joan, cannot finish her education in Goa because she wants to go to the

---
[7] D'Souza, "Back to the Village," 14
[8] *ibid.*

university to study English literature. Her parents, however, believe she will be getting married soon so they pressure her to study teaching instead.[9]

Representing the viewpoint of the younger generation, Joan's cousin, Anita, encourages her to pursue her education in spite of her parent's wishes: "If you can do anything about it, go back. You will stagnate here. What future do I have? Make the best marriage possible, and then settle down into a dull domesticity. Don't fall for that."[10]

Anita knows that her father also abhors city life and believes that a "back to nature move" to a Goan village would be enriching for the family. For the children who are accustomed to life in a large cosmopolitan city, however, it would be a dull and boring life.[11]

Jacob represents the view of an older generation and is convinced that even with the problems of not having access to good educational facilities, public transportation, medical care and electricity, moving back to Goa is the right decision for the family because it is a tie to their ancestral roots. After he notifies his mother about his plans, his return to Goa becomes important news in the village.

To the people in the village, his return is exciting; they have a wonderful time speculating about his reasons for returning and whether he is going to rebuild or extend the ancestral home.

After the family arrives in Goa, Jacob's children, who are not accustomed to village life and the concomitant lack of privacy, are annoyed that they cannot unpack because friends and neighbours constantly drop by to greet them. While Jacob is happy to be back in Goa, he is devastated when he overhears Anita and Joan discussing how traditional their fathers are and how village life is dull and mun-

---

[9]D'Souza, ibid., 24-25
[10]*ibid.*, 30
[11]*ibid.*

dane. To Jacob, living in his family's ancestral home is an essential part of his identity and he cannot understand the feelings of his children.

Another story by J.P. D'Souza that emphasizes the importance of the ancestral home is *The Ruined House*. It depicts the deterioration of an ancestral house and what happened to the children who were supposed to carry on the legacy.

James, the main character, becomes interested in a ruined house, and decides to research the reasons the family allowed the house to fall apart. He is puzzled because he remembers that when he was a child the house was beautiful and people lived in it. He is shocked that something so precious to a Goan family would fall into such awful condition:

> In traditional societies, to maintain the family continuity was almost a duty. Was that not the reason marriage and children loomed so large in the lives of people in these societies even when they knew it was no bed of roses?[12]

The story implies that because the three children never married, the family disintegrated. The eldest son became a drunk, the daughter was spoiled and treated every potential suitor as if he were not good enough for her, and the youngest son was intimidated by the older brother. The author sets forth the traditional view that Goans should marry, live, and keep up the ancestral home-place. In his opinion, if Goans do not marry and raise a family, then their home, as well as their identity, will disintegrate.

In a novel with a theme similar to that in Chinua Achebe's *Things Fall Apart*, the disintegration of a traditional village lifestyle is explored in Pundalik N. Naik's *The Upheaval/Acchev*.

When an outsider from Gujarat comes to the village with an offer of a "better way of life", namely, the opening of a mine, the resultant changes cause the village to disinte-

---

[12] D'Souza, "The Ruined House," 40.

grate. Past rituals become meaningless, children fail to attend school because of the easy money to be earned working in the mine, the daughter of the family becomes self-centered and lazy, the son moves out, doesn't marry and spends his money on alcohol and prostitutes.

The man who brought the mine to the town rapes the daughter, symbolising the rape and loss of dignity to the family. Morals decline to an extent that would be unthinkable in previous times, and leave the parents poor and unable to work. The message is clear: disintegration of the old lifestyle wreaks havoc on the family and is destructive to the village as well.

Frank Simoes' *Glad Seasons in Goa*, has a theme similar to J.P. D'Souza's *"The Village Home."*

The author returns to Goa in the early nineties after living in Bombay and working as a journalist and advertising professional. He declares that his book is "a personal memoir, no more. It is an account of a lifetime's odyssey, in the discovery of my ancestral roots and heritage."[13]

Unlike D'Souza's story though, Simoes does not have an ancestral family home, so he decides to build one, a simple beach hut. He gives a humorous account of his decision to buy land, have it blessed and build a house. His wife Gita and their architect, Sanju, are not impressed with his plans and design the house without consulting him.

The architect insists on reading everything Simoes had ever written about Goa and his family. She declares: "A house should be built with the belief that it will last forever. It should be the way you are, the way you feel about life, and each other."[14] In other words, he has to have family tradition associated with it and build a house filled with his heirlooms that can be inherited by his children. Simoes does

---

[13]Simoes, *Glad Seasons in Goa*, xiii.
[14]*ibid.*, 66.

not resist. The implication is clear; a family home, no matter how it is acquired, is an essential part of any Goan's identity.

In the story "*Dust*" by Heta Pandit, the Goan feeling of connection to the family home and with their ancestors is vividly presented. The time period is not revealed, but it is probably before Liberation.

The main character in the story, Felicia, an unmarried older woman, does her own dusting and refuses to allow the servants to do this chore.[15] While she is dusting, the past merges with the present and the ancestors become part of her daily life as she speaks to the ghosts.

The problem is that most of her ancestors speak Portuguese, while she, on her father's insistence, had received an English education. Her Uncle Fedor did not forgive her for "not learning the language of the colonies."[16]

Felicia agrees that an education in English has created problems for her, not only in communicating with her relatives, but also by hurting her marriage prospects. Luckily, she inherited her house so she still has her connection to her ancestors.

The story reveals the view that the ancestral home is the key to holding on to Goan traditions. "*Dust*" also points out the consequences of breaking from tradition and accepting a culture and language that is foreign to Goa; Felicia is unmarried and cannot communicate with the past.

Exile and return

SINCE World War II, there has been a high rate of Goan emigration to further their education and seek employment. Some Goans have gone to live in Bombay, but many others have gone to the Middle East (the Gulf area which

---

[15] Pandit, "*Dust*," 23.
[16] *ibid.*

includes countries such as Bahrain and Kuwait), the UK, Canada, Africa, Australia and the United States.

Goa's high rate of emigration has had a major impact on Goan identity. Expatriates often write about their experiences in both fiction and non-fiction. Writing about their homeland is a way of holding on to culture and heritage. Eusebio L. Rodrigues believes a Goan is "an Exile in his own land."[17] The Hindu Goan has strong ties with his brothers outside of Goa and the Christian Goan has strong ties with other Christians, especially in the West. He believes that Goans as a group have always felt more comfortable in the West or in places that have "pockets of Western culture".[18]

There was, however, a homeland to which they could always return:

> For the Goan in exile today the distance from Goa is immense – in two ways... physical and psychological. Our sons and daughters, our grandsons and granddaughters find it difficult, almost impossible, to retain Goa in their being. The ties are too thin, stretched out, and will soon break up and be lost. It is and will be very difficult to bring the Goans together as a group – the old Goan village associations no longer have the cohesive power to create and maintain a sense of Goanness. [However] more than others he can adjust to the situation he finds himself in. There is a danger, however, in his very adaptability ....in a generation or two he may lose his Goanness completely.[19]

According to Robert S. Newman, "[t]he experience of Diaspora, of being a total stranger in a strange land, has quintessentially been a Goan experience. Goa along with

---

[17]Rodrigues, "*Stray Thoughts*," 52.
[18]*ibid*.
[19]*ibid.*, 56-57.

Greece, Ireland, Malta, Lebanon and some small Pacific states must have one of the highest rates of migration in the world."[20]

Newman also states that dreaming about Goa and wanting to return to their homeland is to be expected, it is an essential part of Goan life and it helps Goans to deal with the pain and difficulties of family separations.[21]

An examination of Goan literature written by both expatriates and those remaining in Goa reveals a deep desire to return to the ancestral village and home-place. An excellent example of this viewpoint is *On A Goan Beach*, by Remigio Botelho.

A young man, Dom Gomes, returns to Anjuna, Goa, after having lived in Kenya for twenty years. He returns because his father wants him to take care of the family home. The family was in danger of losing their estate in Goa because "...with the departure of the Portuguese from Goa it has become a little difficult for Goans domiciled abroad to come in possession of land or other property."[22]

Dom's father informs his son that if their estate is not being taken care of by an heir, it will pass on to their tenants. He is also concerned about the unstable situation in Africa and believes that the ancestral home would be a comfortable place in which to retire. The family is further concerned that numerous nephews were trying to get the estate because the only person looking after it is an elderly unmarried aunt.[23]

Dom agrees to return to Goa because he is a high school drop out and cannot obtain a good job in Africa. When he arrives in Anjuna in the late sixties or early seventies, he finds that his elderly aunt is not living in the house, but the caretaker Kunti is in charge.

---

[20] Newman, "Goddess of Dreams," 89.
[21] *ibid.*
[22] Botelho, *On A Goan Beach*, 15.
[23] *ibid.*, 14-15.

Dom is shocked when he goes inside the house to discover the extent of its deterioration. "As he moved inside, the area of the corridors, and the rooms confirmed his first impression of that mansion's size, but the extent of neglect and decay was equally vast."[24]

Kunti convinces Dom that he belongs in the home and he should try to make himself worthy of his heritage. Dom's aunt, a lady with very traditional ideas about marriage and family, believes that living up to his heritage means not only looking after the ancestral home, but also marrying a woman from a background of which she approves. She tells Dom that the family disapproved of his father's marriage; he married beneath his status because his bride's mother was the daughter of a musician. The disapproval was so great that the couple were forced to leave Goa and live in Africa.

The aunt is convinced that Dom's father will suffer because of his marriage. She declares, "The souls of our ancestors will never forgive him for what he did. I'm sure he is trying to make up for it now; otherwise he would not have sent you home."[25]

In traditional Goan society, making a bad marriage is a person's social undoing. Approval by the ancestors is important because it shows that the ties to the home-place extend well beyond an individual's choices; they extend into eternity.

One of the themes found in *Tivolem* by Victor Rangel-Ribeiro is the return to the village by a man who has made his fortune while living abroad.

In this novel, the character Senhor Eusebio returns from the Persian Gulf where he worked as a clerk and became wealthy. He decides to retire in his ancestral village, but when he sees his small and cramped ancestral home again,

---

[24] Botelho, *loc. cit.*, 26.
[25] *ibid.*, 48.

he decides to search for another home; one that would show the community that he is wealthy.

Unable to find a suitable house, Senhor Eusebio decides to build one. Land, however, is not readily available. The property he believes would be perfect for his new house belongs to Dona Esmeralda, a woman from an elite family. Senhor Eusebio decides the best approach to buy this land is to approach Dona Elena, a friend of Dona Esmeralda.

She informs him that it will be difficult to buy any land in the area because most people there would never sell their land: "There are sentimental attachments that develop... and reluctances. Status – you'll understand....It's not like selling off a bit of furniture, though heaven knows that can be traumatic. But there are roots and memories...."[26]

Senhor Eusebio quickly tells her that he is not interested in purchasing her land, but rather he wants to buy some of Dona Esmeralda's. He knows she is having financial problems and he is willing to pay a fair price for it.

A meeting with Dona Esmeralda is arranged to discuss his proposal. At first she is reluctant to sell any of her property because she is afraid that her tenants will be forced to move. After negotiating with Dona Esmeralda and agreeing that the tenants can stay, Senhor Eusebio buys the property and builds his "ancestral" house.

Deciding that his new house should show off his newly acquired wealth, but conscious of social sensibilities, he builds a house that is bigger than Dona Elena's but smaller than Dona Esmeralda's. Dona Esmeralda does not approve of Senhor Eusebio's large house and voices her displeasure, saying it is "An ugly monstrosity. It doesn't belong. The man has much money but absolutely no taste."[27]

Dona Elena replies, "Let's thank God for the money and

---

[26] Rangel-Ribeiro, *Tivolem*, 37
[27] *ibid.*, 41

blame the bad taste on the devil."[28] Senhor Eusebio continues to shock Dona Esmeralda by enlarging his plans to add a terrace on the roof with enough room for a band to perform. The tension between the two characters increases as they trade insults such as saying that the other one's roof leaks during the monsoon season and that the antiques in the house are probably fake.[29]

It is ironic that both houses have leaky roofs during the monsoon season, but, fittingly, Senhor Eusebio's new house has more leaks than Dona Esmeralda's. Dona Esmeralda finally decides that insults are not sufficient to punish Senhor Eusebio for trying to upset the social structure in the village; she ostracizes him.

The disapproval of the new house symbolizes the disapproval of the *nouveau riche* returning to Goa believing that they can buy a higher social status. If wealthy people could purchase an elite status, then the traditional elite would lose not only their status, but also their roots, and the established social order would be upset.

An example of Goan literature that discusses the Goan diaspora and the advantages for Goans of keeping their heritage is Lino Leitao's short story, "Thanks to the Goa Bus System." It is interesting to note that the late Lino Leitao himself was part of the Goan diaspora; till his recent death, he was resident in Canada.

"*Thanks to the Goa Bus System*" is a short story about Angelo Martins, a Goan who emigrates to Canada. Before he leaves, he promises his mother that he will marry a woman not only Goan, but also from the same caste.

After arriving in Canada, he adapts very well to his new culture. He learns both English and French and becomes a Canadian citizen. He saves his money and becomes very wealthy, but does not marry because of his promise to his

---

[28] Rangel-Ribeiro, *loc. cit.*
[29] *ibid.*, 42-43

mother. Angelo feels uncomfortable asking Goan women in Canada about their backgrounds, so he decides that he should return to Goa to find a wife.

At first it is difficult to find him a suitable wife because the Goan women he meets prefer men who are living in the Middle East and are, therefore, wealthier, rather than those who have been living in Canada. Angelo hears about a girl in Margao through a matchmaker, and decides to take the bus to see her.

While he is on the bus, he discusses politics with other passengers and meets a woman named Vanda, the woman of his dreams. He has lunch with her and decides that she is the girl that he wants to marry. When he returns home, he discovers that his mother not only knows Vanda's family, she also approves of the match. Angelo is happy that he is able to keep his promise to his mother.[30]

The message in this story is clear. Angelo could go to a foreign country and change his citizenship, but he could not change his cultural ties to his homeland. Although he declares he is keeping his promise to his mother by marrying someone of whom she approves, the story ends with him finding the perfect mate and living happily ever after. The clear implication is that sticking to your roots and your heritage will lead you to happiness.

The Mango and the Tamarind Tree by Leslie de Noronha presents the reverse situation. The main character, Raoul, returns home from abroad during the time of the Liberation. He falls in love with a girl from an unsuitable family, but the romance does not end happily. Raoul is from a very upper class elite family with a long history in the community and an ancestral home full of antiques. When he first arrives home he notices there are new neighbours next door. He asks his mother about these new neighbours and she responds:

---

[30] Leitao, "Goa Bus System," 68

[they are] 'The Gonsalves family.'

'Never heard of them. Who are they?' Raoul asked.

'You don't know them,' his mother replied....

'Yes, but who are they? New neighbours?'

'Not quite. They have been here almost a year, but I never asked them over. The father is a retired engineer or architect or something. They made a lot of money during the war in British Africa; Kenya, I think. They went out several years ago and have returned to Anjolim from where they originally came. So they are local people, of sorts, but a trifle common.'[31]

Raoul's mother clearly shows that she has investigated the family's background and lineage and she does not consider them to be socially acceptable. Although the Gonsalves family may be well educated and have become wealthy by going abroad, they were still not accepted by the elites because wealth and education have not removed the stigma of their lack of social status.

When Raoul meets the Gonsalves family, he immediately falls in love with their daughter, Estelle. Raoul's family is horrified by the romance and tries to arrange a marriage for him with a "suitable girl" from his caste, but he is not interested in any of the girls they choose for him.

Raoul also breaks tradition not only by refusing to go through an arranged marriage, but also by deciding that he does not want the ancestral home when his mother dies. The family is again horrified and they remind him that the ancestral home is family property. The priest, Father Couto, speaks to Raoul about selling the house:

'What's this I hear about selling Anjolim, the house and all the property. Is it true Raoul?'

---

[31]Noronha, *The Mango and Tamarind Tree*, 48

'Yes and no. I have been thinking about it.'
'It is family property.'
'I know.' Raoul said, slightly bitter. 'That point has been repeated *ad nauseum*.'[32]

Raoul and Estelle's romance ends unhappily when she chooses to take care of her disabled younger brother rather than marry Raoul.[33] The message conveyed is that choosing an unsuitable partner and giving up the ancestral home – both of which are acts of giving up one's roots and heritage – will leave Goans disappointed and broken-hearted. In this and many other stories, choosing a suitable life partner and raising a family in the ancestral home is one's ultimate goal in life. It is an obligation that is not to be taken lightly because it reaches to the very essence of Goan identity.

Some Goans who emigrate however, do establish roots outside of Goa, but Goa still remains not only in their hearts, but also an essential part of their identity.

Peter Nazareth's novel *The General Is Up*, set in the fictitious country of Damibia – which in reality is the country of Uganda – explores the situation of Goans in Africa. It is interesting to note that the author is a Goan from Uganda.

In this novel, The General becomes the dictator of the country and passes a law that anyone who cannot prove that they have Damibian citizenship must leave the country. Many Damibians of Goan descent were born there, but cannot prove their citizenship.[34]

The main character, David Da Costa, is a high government official. Although he was born and raised in Africa, he is also a member of the Goan Association. He thinks of himself as a Goan/Damibian.[35] The problem is that although his brother can prove citizenship, he cannot.

---

[32] Noronha, *op. cit.*, 171
[33] *ibid.*, 224
[34] Nazareth, *General Is Up*, 33-37
[35] *ibid.*

This presents a huge dilemma for those who cannot prove Damibian citizenship because they are not considered to be British citizens; in reality, they are stateless people. Some of the Goan-Africans who lose their citizenship choose to emigrate back to Goa and some choose to go to England, but the majority receive refugee status in Canada.[36]

David is forced to leave Damibia to live in Canada, but he does not resign from his government position until after he is safely out of the country.[37] It is interesting to note that Damibian Goans did not emigrate to Bombay or other parts of India. *The General Is Up* shows that the Goan diaspora is increasing and Goans now live all over the world. Although Goans have established roots outside of Goa many still consider themselves Goans no matter where they are residing.

Eusebio L. Rodrigues' essay, *"Thoughts on Exile,"* discusses the plight of Goans who were in Uganda and were then expelled from the country. He states that Goans generally did not leave Goa as refugees, nor because they were fleeing political or religious persecution. They went to Africa or Bombay with dreams that they would return to get married and to retire: "The Goan dream was not to settle in a foreign land. It was to work hard, earn money, save it in order to return to Goa."[38]

Rodrigues points out that the Goans in Africa were different from other Goans because most of them had emigrated from Goa when it was still a Portuguese colony; therefore, many of the Goans in Kampala thought of themselves as Portuguese citizens.[39] The author states, "For me it [the problem of Goans being exiled from Uganda and becoming refugees in another country] provides insights into the problem of being a true Goan."[40]

---

[36]Nazareth, *loc. cit.*, 111-116.
[37]*ibid.*, 106.
[38]Rodrigues, Thoughts on Exile, 53
[39]*ibid.*, 54
[40]*ibid.*

Although Goan emigration is a popular subject in Goan literature, very little is written about individual Goan women who emigrate, as opposed to the whole family.

"*Gulf*" by Heta Pandit explores a woman's experience of leaving her daughter to go to work in the Gulf. Olinda Rosario, a poor woman who is fifty-three years old, is offered a job by her *bhatkar* to work as a nanny for his daughter who is going to the Gulf with her husband and three small children.[41] She is surprised to be offered the job because she believes that it is a good position. She dreams of the wealth she will acquire by working abroad:

> Think of it! With money she'd buy all the gold in the world. She'd cover her little Samantha [Olinda's daughter] with gold – kilos, tons of it. She looked at the landlord's daughter... Olinda thought of each of her neighbours. Now she'd show them! She would also come back with glossy, shiny net saris for Samantha.[42]

Unfortunately Olinda does not realize that she obtained this position because the family believes it does not have to pay her much money. She also has no idea as to the working conditions she is going to encounter overseas. In reality, the family will treat her like a slave:

> Hazel [the *bhatkar*'s daughter] had decided that she would explain the rules of the house after they got there.... she had not told her that she would have to keep the house scrupulously clean, get the children dressed for school, give their breakfasts, cook their lunches, prepare their teas, and have them bathed and dressed for dinners. That there would be no Sundays and no holidays... and that she would not be allowed to

---

[41] Pandit. "The Gulf," The author includes a glossary at the back of the book where she defines *bhatkar* as a Konkani word meaning the "landed gentry in Goa."

[42] *ibid.*, 190.

> travel on her own... that she would not be given an allowance but that her remittances would be sent directly to the bank here [in Goa] ... that she could only return after three whole years. That during that time, she would have no friends, no contact with anybody.[43]

This short story illustrates the problems many Goan women encounter when they leave Goa to work abroad. Many of the women who leave Goa do so not to further their educations, but to work as domestics in the homes of wealthy families. Many of them must emigrate in order to support family members, especially their children.

Although these women dream about becoming wealthy and returning to Goa, for most their dream will be unfulfilled.

Exploring the writings of Goan authors, one realizes that the concept that one must return is particularly strong among the expatriate community. Peter Nazareth believes that "the Portuguese conquest of the city-state of Goa led to a long displacement that has not ended. Various things lie submerged in the Goan unconscious. First there is pre-Portuguese Hinduism, and second:

> Goans have gone all over the world, and while they have longed for home, they have adapted to their new environments and taken new things into the matrix of their culture. The people who have done it best may not have been intellectuals but 'ordinary' women who have had it imprinted on them – thanks to dozens of uprisings against the Portuguese which failed and led to the men being punished–it is up to them to look after the future of their children.[44]

---

[43]Pandit, *op.cit.*, 192-193.
[44]Nazareth, "End of Exile," 40.

Nazareth raises the questions asked by many people: "Why do Goans insist they are Goan? Why don't you say you are Indian? Isn't Goa part of India?" to explain the role Goan writers play:

> The explanation is from our history: Goans have been so denationalized by colonialism that we dig in to resist further denial that we are a people. The fact we can provide so little evidence to show why we are particularly proud to be Goans proves my point.[45]

In the words of Eusebio L. Rodrigues: "Today's Goans are experiencing an exile that is an essential part of the human condition. We sense that we are all wanderers on this earth. That we are far from home."[46]

This sense of alienation is also present in many Goan works of fiction. They present conflicting ideas between the generations; the older people want to maintain the traditional values and the younger people want to live their lives according to their own ideas. The more this identity is challenged, however, the more the older generation will want to define it.

Children are learning Konkani and the ancestral village and home continues to hold a special place in Goan consciousness for those who remain in Goa. For those who have moved abroad, it is inevitable, however, that the more the Diaspora increases, and the more generations are removed from their Goan roots, there will be less interest that Goans' descendants will have in returning to Goa. They will have no emotional ties to the village and the ancestral home.

---

[45] Nazareth, *loc. cit.*, 46.
[46] Rodrigues, "Stray Thoughts," 58

Chapter 6

Changing identity

GOAN IDENTITY has changed dramatically since Goa became part of India. While most Goans have given up their Portuguese identity and no longer claim to be Portuguese or Portuguese citizens, many have retained some of the Portuguese language and culture. Most Goans today have adopted a dual Goan/Indian identity which is similar to the sub-nationality view of Puerto Ricans. The question is: can Goan identity be defined as a sub-nationality or a completely separate identity?

One example of a colony that has formed a sub-nationality, or, as some scholars argue, a separate identity from its colonial power is Puerto Rico. How do Puerto Ricans view themselves? Are they Americans first? Puerto Ricans first? Or only Puerto Ricans?

The Puerto Rican Nation on the Move, Identities on the Island and the United States, by Jorge Duany, discusses how nations and nationalism cannot be treated only as a political ideology; the issues must also be considered a cultural phenomena. According to Duany, Puerto Ricans do have the view that they share the same religion, language, and cultural customs that make them different from non-Puerto Rican Americans.

Yet, although Puerto Rico has been a colony of the United States (officially, a self-governing unincorporated territory of the US) since 1917, Puerto Ricans do not have the perception that they are Puerto Ricans first, then Americans second. According to Duany, "most Puerto Ricans see no contradiction between asserting their Puerto Rican nationality at the same time defending their US citizenship."[1]

But Puerto Rican identity does not remain the same, over time it changes according to the perception of its people: "All forms of identity are imagined, invented and represented...."[2]

Duany further states that, "nations are not natural and eternal essences but contingent, slippery and fuzzy constructs, always in a process of redefinition."[3] This is consistent with my finding that in Goan literature, and also in the thoughts of others on the subject, Goans have also changed their perception of their identity over time.

A second important issue in defining Goan identity has been the debate over the official language of Goa. Since the Official Language Act, however, most Goans agree that Konkani should be the official language. The majority of Goans believe that using Marathi instead of Konkani would mean that Goa would lose its unique identity and would just become a district of Maharashtra. Although the issue about the official language is supposedly settled, Goans are increasingly learning English because they believe that it is the language of success.

The concept of Goan identity is in transition. As more Goans leave the region in search of educational and employment opportunities, it has become important for them to maintain the dream of returning to their homeland. The dream, however, is more than just returning home. It in-

---

[1] Duany, *Puerto Rican Nation*, 13.
[2] *ibid.*, 8.
[3] *ibid.*, 7.

cludes creating, maintaining, or acquiring a home not only for oneself, but also for one's descendants.

In other words, it is important for Goans to define and preserve their heritage, traditions, and distinct culture. It does seem, however, that they are ignoring the reality that the Goa of their dreams is changing dramatically. It is gradually assuming an Indian identity as they have swapped one colonial ruler for another. Only time will tell how well Goans are able to preserve a separate identity as more Indian influences seep into their culture.

While there are differences of opinion about how Goans define themselves, they believe that their traditions and culture must be preserved. Many Goans believe they will lose their traditions as the Diaspora grows and people – such as Kashmiris, Gypsies, and Rajasthanis, among others – migrate to Goa in search of jobs.[4]

The Indian government and tourist industry officials have also attempted to define Goan Identity. They have not always been accurate. As Goa becomes more of an international vacation destination, these officials sell to unsuspecting tourists what they have defined as authentic Goan culture. Many emphasize Goa's Europeanized culture while ignoring the region's Indian and Hindu history. Goa has become a "Touristan" for Europeans who go to Goa not to learn and explore the history and culture of a unique region of India, but, rather, just to enjoy the beaches.

Many of the Goans who return as tourists and bring their families, however, are interested in Goan history and culture. As a result, the Diaspora is starting to have significant impact on the tourist industry. A positive aspect of it is that the relationship between the local population and visitors to Goa continues its ties to the West:

> Perhaps such knowledge of and connections with, the wider world also contribute to the rela-

---

[4]Wilson, "Paradoxes of Tourism," 203

tively cosmopolitan atmosphere in Goa.... The positive reinterpretation of their colonial past seems to have prevented the growth of the sort of resentments which are common throughout the Caribbean. Nor did there seem to be any of the confusion between memories of colonial servility and ideas of customer service which also generate tension and hostility between local inhabitants and tourists in the West Indies.[5]

One of the best ways to see how Goans view themselves and the changes their identity has undergone is to read their literature. Most of their novels, short stories, plays, and essays contain descriptions of how they define their identity. Newspapers, periodicals, and internet bulletin boards also provide a great deal of information on Goan identity. These additional sources also provide Goans from many different professions an opportunity to express their views, and thereby allow for a more complete view of how Goan identity is perceived and how it is changing.

Goa has the potential to turn into a tourist destination in which the indigenous identity will be preserved and celebrated in a way that is similar to the Mayan culture of the Yucatan peninsula in Southern Mexico. In the Yucatan, the Mexican government has spent millions of dollars renovating ancient sites which now provide employment to a formerly impoverished indigenous people, while at the same time validating their heritage in the world.[6]

As a result, the area has a dynamic living culture which takes great pride in the quality of the services it provides. Eugenio Cruz, an indigenous tour guide in Mexico who is very proud of his heritage and work, states that becoming a guide is not an easy task to accomplish. Even if guides work for private companies, they must pass rigorous government

---

[5]Wilson, "Paradoxes of Tourism," 190
[6]INEGI website.

exams on Mexican history, culture, and art. He explains that even the groundskeepers of ancient sites must pass these exams.[7]

Some guides are graduate history students or professors who work in the tourism industry during the summer. Other guides are native Mayans from the Yucatan who tell traditional stories associated with the ancient ruins. These guides are very popular with the children who visit the area. Most guides speak both Spanish and English, in addition to Mayan, and many of them also speak European languages such as French and German. They are all enthusiastic in sharing their heritage with visitors.

A similar situation has occurred in Madeira, the island region of Portugal; it is located west of Morocco in the Atlantic Ocean. Madeira, though, was not technically a colony, and it was not settled until 1418 when João Gonçalves Zarco and Tristão Vaz Texeira accidentally landed on these islands when they were sailing to Africa. They found these islands deserted. Madeira (the Portuguese word for "wood") acquired its name because it was heavily forested. The forests were stripped, sugar plantations were built, and the capital city Funchal became an important international seaport for the Portuguese to use on their way to Portuguese colonies.

During the seventeenth century, Madeira abandoned growing sugarcane and started to make wine; even today, the island is famous all over the world for its wine. In the nineteenth century tourism was added and it has become an essential part of the Madeiran economy.

In 1891 the Reid hotel in Funchal opened to cater to British tourists. Today British tourists are still flocking to Madeira. There are many charter flights from England and most people on the island speak English.[8]

Like Goa, Madeira also has a Diaspora. Madeirans,

---

[7]Eugenio Cruz, personal interview.
[8]Dunlap, *Traveler Portugal*, 221.

however, often return to use their newly acquired language skills in a highly regulated tourism industry. Taxi drivers in Madeira often are hired by the day as tour guides and they are usually as knowledgeable as the tour guides who work for private companies.[9]

In Goa, the people are equally proud of their history and heritage, but the exiled Goans are not given an incentive to return home other than an emotional attachment to their former village and home-place. Although there are many historic and culturally important sites, temples and archaeological places of importance, they are not well developed for tourism.

If Goans can present their culture and traditions in a manner similar to that of the Yucatan or Madeira, revenue from the tourist industry will provide employment to the returnees and other Goans, and also assist in raising funds for preserving their museums, ancient sights, and traditions.

A few tour companies have already come up with the idea of comparing Goan tourism to that of the Yucatan as Goan charms are now advertised as "nearly Mexican."[10]

Mexico has a very diverse and different culture from Goa; such advertising does a disservice to both areas, and revives the argument set forth in the *Denationalisation of Goans* that Goa does not have its own unique culture and identity. While the Diaspora has helped Goans to develop a more cosmopolitan identity, they should take steps to preserve their unique Goan identity before it is lost forever or completely absorbed by the wider reality of India.

---

[9]Catling, Top 10 Madeira, 103.
[10]Newman, Goa: Transformation, 32.

Chapter 7

References

Abbas, K.A. *Maria*. New Delhi: Hind Pocket Books, 1971.

Achebe, Chinua. *Things Fall Apart*. New York: Doubleday, 1994.

Anderson, Benedict. *Imagined Communities: Reflections on the Origin and Spread of Nationalism*. New York: Verso, 1991.

Angle, Prabhakar. "A Culture 'Conceived' and Misconceived". In *The Transforming of Goa*. Mapusa, Goa: Other India Press, 1999.

— — —. *Goa: An Economic Update*. Bombay: Goa Hindu Association Kala Vibhag, 2001.

— — —. *Goa: Concepts and Misconcepts*. Bombay: The Goan Hindu Association, 1994.

Apechu, William. "Fire". Entry posted February 10, 2003. "CyberVoices: Topic of Discussion: Saving Heritage. Re: Goa for Konkani!! Konkani for Goa!!" *Navhind Times on the Web*. http://navhindtimes.com/cybervoices/messages/314.htm (accessed May 14, 2005).

Ashcroft, Bill, Gareth Griffiths, and Helen Tiffin. *Key Concepts in Post-Colonial Studies*. New York: Rutledge, 1998.

Bhat, Ravikant Anand. Entry posted March 22, 2003. "CyberVoices: Topic of Discussion: Saving Heritage. Re: Language Controversy" *Navhind Times on the Web*. http://navhindtimes.com/cybervoices/messages/359.htm (accessed May 14, 2005).

Bradnock, Robert and Roma Bradnock. *Goa Handbook*. Chicago: Passport Books, 1997.

Boman-Behram, B.K. *Goa and Ourselves*. Bombay: Boman-Behram, 1955.

Botelho, Remigio. *On A Goan Beach*. Panjim: Star Types, 1994.

Burde, Nikhil. Entry posted on March 26, 2003 "Cyber Voices.". "CyberVoices: Topic of Discussion: Saving Heritage. Re: Primary Education Should be in Konkani: CM *Navhind Times on the Web*. http://navhindtimes.com/cybervoices-/messages/374.htm (accessed on May 14, 2005)

Catling, Christopher. *Top 10 Madeira*. Eyewitness Top 10 Travel Guides. London: Dorling Kindersley, 2005.

Chandler, Liza Prado and Gary Prado Chandler. *Yucatan Peninsula*. 8th ed. Moon Handbooks. Emeryville, CA: Avalon Travel, 2005.

Childs, Peter, and Patrick Williams. *An Introduction to Post-Colonial Theory*. New York: Prentice Hall, 1997.

Correia Afonso, John S. J. "To Cherish and to Share: The Goan Christian Heritage". *Goa: Continuity and Change*. Toronto: University of Toronto, 1995.

Coutinho, João da Veiga. *A Kind of Absence: Life in the Shadow of History*. New Haven: Yuganta Press, 1997.

Couto, Maria Aurora. Foreword. *The Upheaval/Acchev*, by Pundalik N. Naik. trans. Vidya Pai. New Delhi: Oxford University Press, 2002. xi-xxxi.

Cruz, Eugenio. Personal interview, April 15, 2002.

D'Souza, Carmo. *Angela's Goan Identity*. Mapusa, Goa: GKP Constructions, 1994.

D'Souza, J.P. "Back to the Village." *The Village Home and Other Stories*. Mumbai: Michael Lobo Publishers, 1998.

— — —. "The Ruined House." *The Village Home and Other Stories*. Mumbai: Michael Lobo Publishers, 1998.

Dantas, Norman. Introduction. *The Transforming of Goa*. Mapusa: Other India Press, 1999. 1-4.

Danvers, Frederick Charles. *The Portuguese in India*. 2 vols. New Delhi: Asian Educational Services, 1992.

Davila, Arleene. *Sponsored Identities: Cultural Politics in Puerto Rico*. Philadelphia: Temple University Press, 1997.

Duany, Jorge. *The Puerto Rican Nation on the Move: Identities on the Island in the United States.* Chapel Hill: University of North Carolina Press, 2002.

De Mascarenhas, Telo. *When the Mango Trees Blossomed.* Bombay: Orient Longman, 1976.

De Noronha, Leslie *The Mango and the Tamarind Tree.* Calcutta: Writers Workshop, 1970.

De Sousa, Nora Secco. "Konknni: My Mother Tongue." *Goa Cradle of my Dreams.* Pilar: Xaverian Press, n.d.

De Souza, Teotonio. entry posted January 2001. "Goan Identity: One, Many or None." Goacom.com http://www.goacom.com/goanow/2001/jan/goanidentity.html (accessed May 20, 2004.)

Diniz-Dourdil, Julio. *"In Search of Identity."* Goan Overseas Digest. 8.4 (Oct-Dec 2000): 4-5.

Dunlop, Fiona. *National Geographic Traveler Portugal.* Washington: National Geographic Society, 2005.

Drucker, Margaret Roberts. *Mangoes and Chappaties.* New York: Vantage Press, 1999.

Faleiro, Luizinho. *My Goa: An Autobiography.* Margao: Dr. Francisco Luis Gomes Memorial Trust, 1999.

Fanon, Frantz. *Black Skin White Masks.* New York: Grove Press, 1967.

George, Niraj. entry posted on February 03, 2005. "CyberVoices: Topic of Discussion: Saving Heritage. Re: Goa for Konkani!! Konkani for Goa!!" *Navhind Times on the Web.* http://navhindtimes.com/cybervoices/messages/299.htm (accessed May 14, 2005).

Goa Congress Committee, *The Denationalisation of Goans.* Bombay: Padma Publications, 1944.

Gomes, Olivinho J.F. *Village Goa (A Study of Goan Social Structure and Change).* New Delhi: Chand & Company, 1987.

Henry, Joseph K. "On the Mango and the Tamarind Tree." *Journal of South Asian Literature,* Vol VIII No 01 (Winter Spring 1983): 13-16.

Hobgood, John. "Defining Goans and Their Culture." *Goa: Continuity and Change.* Toronto: University of Toronto, 1995.

Instituto Nacional de Estadistica de Geografia e Informatica. http://www.inegi.gob.mx

Kamat, Sharmila. "Tongue of Violence." *Mango Mood*. Panaji: Self Published, 1995.

Larsen, Karin. *Faces of Goa*. New Delhi: Gyan Publishing, 1998.

Leitao, Lino. "Thanks to the Goan Bus System." *Six Tales*. Cornwall, ON: Vesta Publications, 1980.

Lobo, Jorge Ataide. *Liberation: A Novel*. Panaji: Casa J.D. Fernandes, 1971.

Madeira's Official Tourism Website. http://www.madeiratourism.org.

Mankekar, D.R. *The Goa Action*. Bombay: Popular Book Depot, 1962.

Mascarenhas, Lambert. *Sorrowing Lies My Land*. Mapusa, Goa: Other India Press, 1999.

— — —. *The Greater Tragedy*. Dona Paula, Goa: Lamas Publications, 1988.

Mascarenhas, Margaret. *Skin*. New Delhi: Penguin India, 2001.

Naik, Pundalik. *The Upheaval/Acchev*. Trans.Vidya Pai. New Delhi: Oxford University Press, 2002

Naik, Vinayak, ed. "Marathi? No Way!" *Goa Today*, June 2000, 36-38.

Narayan, Rajan. entry posted on May 20, 2005. "The Essence of Goan Identity." http://www.rajannarayan.com/archive/18-1-2004. (Accessed on May 20, 2005).

Nazareth, Peter. *The General is Up*. Toronto: Tsar Publications, 1991.

— — —. ed, "Introduction." *Journal of South Asian Literature*, Vol VIII No. 01 (Winter, Spring 1983): 1-293.

— — —. "The End of Exile, Or, Why Should Goans Read Goan Literature?". *Goa: Continuity and Change*. Toronto: University of Toronto, 1995.

Newman, Robert S. "Goa: Transformation of an Indian Region." *Of Umbrellas, Goddesses, and Dreams: Essays on Goan Culture and Society*. Mapusa, Goa: Other India Press, 2001.

— — —. Introduction. *Of Umbrellas, Goddesses, and Dreams: Essays on Goan Culture and Society*. Mapusa, Goa: Other India Press, 2001.

— — —. "Konkani Mai Ascends the Throne: The Cultural Basis of Goan Statehood." *Of Umbrellas, Goddesses, and Dreams: Es-*

says on Goan Culture and Society. Mapusa, Goa: Other India Press, 2001.

Nicholson, Louise. *Goa*. New Delhi: Gulmohur Press, 1998.

Pandit, Heta. "Dust". *Dust and other Short Stories from Goa*. Porvorim, Goa: Heritage Network, 2002.

— — —. "The Gulf". *Dust and other Short Stories from Goa*. Porvorim, Goa: Heritage Network, 2002.

Pearson, M.N. *The Indian Ocean (Seas in History)*. New York: Routledge, 2003.

— — —. *The Portuguese in India*. New York: Cambridge University Press, 1987.

Peres Da Costa, Suneeta. *Homework*. New York: Bloomsbury Publishing, 1999.

Priolkar, A.K. *Goa: Facts versus Fiction*. Poona: Smt. Sudha Joshi, 1962.

— — —. "Who is a Goan?" *Journal of South Asian Literature*, Vol VIII No 01 (Winter, Spring 1983): 269-271.

Raposo, Romeo. entry posted on Feb 03, 2003. "CyberVoices: Topic of Discussion: Saving Heritage. Re: Language Controversy" *Navhind Times on the Web.* http://navhindtimes.com-/cybervoices/messages/301.htm (accessed on May 14, 2005).

Rangel-Ribeiro, Victor. Email interview. September 15, 2001.

— — —. *Tivolem*. Minneapolis: Milkweed Editions, 1998.

Rodrigues, Eusebio. "Stray Thoughts on Goan Exile." *Goa: Continuity and Change*. Toronto: University of Toronto, 1995.

Rubinoff, Arthur G. *The Construction of a Political Community: Integration and Identity in Goa*. Thousand Oaks, CA: Sage Publications, 1998.

Rubinoff, Janet Ahner. "The Casteing of Catholicism: Goan Responses to Conversion." *Goa: Continuity and Change*. Toronto: University of Toronto, 1995.

Said, Edward. *Orientalism*. New York: Vintage Books, 1979.

Saksena, R.N. *Goa: Into the Mainstream*. New Delhi: Abhinav Publications, 1974.

Santa Rita Vas, Luis. Introduction. *Modern Goan Short Stories* Mumbai: Jaico Publishing, 2002. vii-x.

Sardessai, ManoharRai. *A History of Konkani Literature*. New Delhi: Sahitya Akademi, 2000.

Shetty, Manohar. Introduction *Ferry Crossing: Short Stories from Goa*. New Delhi: Penguin India, 1998. xi-xviii.

Shirodkar, P.P. *Goa's Struggle for Freedom*. Panaji: Ajanta Publications, 1988.

Simoes, Frank. *Glad Seasons in Goa*. New Delhi: Penguin Books, 1994.

Wagle, Narendra and George Coelho, eds. *Goa: Continuity and Change*. Toronto: University of Toronto, 1995.

Wilson, David. "Paradoxes of Tourism in Goa." *The Transforming of Goa*. Mapusa, Goa: Other India Press, 1999.

Wyrick, Deborah. *Fanon for Beginners*. New York: Writers and Readers Publishing, 1998.

Chapter 8

Goa in creative writing

An annotated bibliography, compiled by Frederick Noronha and Pamela D'Mello, focussing on creative writing in English.

GOAN WRITING enjoys, at best, only a small and scattered market. This is true of Goan writing in any language, even though there are a plethora of books now emerging from this small region.

Most books – except a few prominent titles – can be difficult to locate too. Since most local publications – newspapers or periodicals – rarely review Goa-related books, there is also little awareness about new books when they are first published.

To further complicate the scenario, by the time the book gets noticed, it is probably out of print, certainly not available in all bookshops, or difficult to locate for other reasons. The fact that books here are often self-published, or brought out by small publishers, means they can be even more difficult to track down

One useful place where one can find Goa-related titles is the quaintly-named Rare Books Section of the Central Library in Panjim. This section is currently located near the Goa Police headquarters, but due to shift to the capital's Pato locality. Under the provisions of law, a publisher is required to 'deposit' three copies here of every new publication that comes out from Goa. So you have a fair chance of finding a Goa-related book you're looking for, including rather early 20th century publications. Once a year, usually in the first quarter, a list of these publications is put out in the State's *Official Gazette*.

Goans have written in diverse languages – 13 according to one count. This makes it difficult, if not impossible, to compare works done in different languages. Besides, only very few books get translated from one language to another. The listing below focuses largely on books available in English.

If interested in collecting Goa-related books: search listings of in-print titles online. Check out Broadway Book Centre (at the end of 18th June Road, near Santa Inez, or at goa-books.com); the Other India Book Store (Mapusa, 2263306, above the Old Mapusa Clinic or otherindiabookstore.com); Hotel Mandovi Bookshop (Panjim); Golden Heart Emporium near the GPO in Margao; or Literati off the Calangute-Candolim main road near the Tarcar Ice Factory. All stock a good selection of Goa-related books.

Lastly, an asterisk (*) mark alongside the book's title in the listing below indicates it is probably out-of-print, or currently not easily available for purchase in Goa.

ANTHOLOGIES

Goan Literature: A Modern Reader.
Peter Nazareth, guest editor, with assistance of Joseph K. Henry.
Journal of South Asian Literature.
Asian Studies Centre. Michigan State University.
Pp 297. Winter-Spring 1983
US ISSN 0091-5637

An early, fascinating view of Goan writing, brought

together by Peter Nazareth, a literature professor in the US who has also described himself as an African writer. Reprinted in Goa in 2010. *Goan Literature: A Modern Reader* contains extracts from novels, essays, poems, short-stories (from 'the outside', and 'local' settings), stories of return, essays on home and exile, a one-act play, and a bibliography and notes on contributors.

Ever since it was first printed, this tome has been very rare and difficult to find in Goa. Yet, this arguably is the single-most important volume that could help one understand 20th century Goa (and earlier phases) in a nutshell.

Among the writers included in this volume are Leslie de Noronha, Orlando da Costa, Lambert Mascarenhas and Peter Nazareth (extracts from novels); Antonio da Cruz, Philip Furtado, ManoharRai Sardessai, Lucio Rodrigues, Alfred F. Braganza, Manuel C. Rodrigues, Ladis da Silva, George Menezes, Wilson Fernandes, Evagrio Jorge, Antonio Menezes, A.K. Priolkar, Marion da Silva (essays); Eunice de Souza, H.O. Nazareth, Raul de L. Furtado, Santan Rodrigues, Raul da Gama Rose, Melanie Silgardo, George Menezes, R.V. Pandit, ManoharRai Sardessai, B.B. Borkar, Robert de Souza, Philip Furtado, Manuel C. Rodrigues, Cyrano Valles, Dom Martin, Olivinho Gomes, Hermogenes Furtado (poems); Raul de L. Furtado, Violet Lannoy Dias, Adelaide de Souza, Lino Leitão, Loy Saldanha, Armando Menezes, Sheela Naik, Avinash Kudchadkar, Lucio Rodrigues, Assagaonkar, Antonio da Cruz, Berta de Menezes Bragança (short stories); Loy Saldanha (one-act play).

It has a stronger focus on writing emerging from the rather-active Goan diaspora. Peter Nazareth's work played an early role in highlighting the existence of Goan writing, which in the 1980s was even more scattered and difficult to find.

Nazareth writes: "And material did come in: from India, Australia, Canada, England, Portugal and elsewhere. Many Goans, like West Indians, were living outside, yearning for home, refusing to be denationalized. I received writing by Goans about Goans, by Goans not about Goans, by non-Goans about Goans, by those who claimed one parent to be Goan, and by someone who had started an organization to trace ancestry through the mother. I discovered that Goans had written in at least thirteen languages, of which the chief were English, Portuguese, Marathi and Konkani. The last of these, the mother tongue, being written in three different scripts...."

This book was originally published as an issue of the *Journal of South Asian Literature* (formerly *MAHFIL*), and has just been republished in Goa.

Ferry Crossing: Short Stories from Goa.
Manohar Shetty (Ed.)
Penguin, New Delhi
Pp 268. Rs 250 (1998)

A newer, more Goa-focussed anthology that includes translated work from the original Konkani writing. It has short stories from Konkani, Marathi, Portuguese and English. Includes the work of Chandrakant Keni, Pundalik Naik, Meena Kakodkar, Mahabaleshwar Sail, Vasant Bhagwant Sawant, Damodar Mauzo, Uday Bhembre, Naresh Kavadi, Vithal Thakur, Subhash Bhende, Laxmanrao Sardessai, Raghunandan V. Kelkar, Orlando da Costa, Vimala Devi, Epitacio Paes, Victor Rangel-Ribeiro, Peter Nazareth, Lambert Mascarenhas, Hubert Ribeiro, E.R.A. da Cunha and Leslie de Noronha.

Reflected in Water: Writings on Goa
Jerry Pinto (ed.)
Penguin Books, New Delhi
Pp 295. Rs 395 (2006)

Journalist and poet Jerry Pinto edited this book – an update to earlier writing and anthologies on Goa – adding to his own work of poetry, and books such as *Surviving Women* (2000), *Helen: The Life and Times of an H-Bomb* (2006) and *Bombay, Meri Jaan: Writings on Mumbai*, which he co-edited with another Goa-linked writer, the *Time Out* (Mumbai) editor Naresh Fernandes.

This book has a wide range of writing – new and old – on Goa, from locals, expats and others who have focussed their attention here. In the last category are William Dalrymple's 'At Dona Georgina's', Graham Green's 'Goa the Unique' and Richard F. Burton's excerpt from *Goa and the Blue Mountains*. Fortyfour essays in all. Varied perspectives; but there could have been more when it comes to representing the varied (and often conflicting) perspectives on this tiny region.

Episódio Oriental: Readings in Indo-Portuguese Literature
Maria Inês Figueira & Óscar de Noronha
Third Millennium, Panjim.
Pp 176, Rs 225 (2007)

English -Portuguese text focussing on the Indo-Portuguese encounter and the literature that emerged. A historical overview of Indo-Portuguese literature (Prof Pratima Kamat), Goa in Portuguese Literature (Maria do Céu Barreto), and a focus on individual writers – Adeodato Barreto, Alvaro da Costa, 'Gip', Fanchu Loyola, Nascimento Mendonça, Luis de Menezes Bragança and Orlando da Costa.

Dicionário de Literatura Goesa *
Aleixo Manuel da Costa
Instituto Cultural de Macau - Fundcão Oriente
Three volumes. (1997)

This three-volume ambitious dictionary seeks to list Goan writing of the past, particularly – but not only – that undertaken in Portuguese. Each author gets listed, together with a brief biographical mention and also a bibliographical note. Specially useful to know about the work done in the past, more so in a Goa where so much has beens lost because of the abrupt changes in languages used here – and also the lack of translations among varied languages. It's amazing how many names, titles of books, facts and information about the writers the former head of Goa's main library managed to collect and collate.

Tiatrancho Jelo
Felicio Cardoso (Ed.)
Goa Konknni Akademi, Ponnji, Gõy
Rs 60 (1996)

A publication in the Romi Konkani. It includes scripts of some prominent *tiatrs*, or Konkani plays. Includes '*Kedna Udetolo To Dis*' (C Alvares), '*Atancho Temp*' (Remmie Colaço), '*23 Vorsam*' (John Claro), '*Vavraddi*' (Prem Kumar), '*Ekuch Rosto*' (M. Boyer).

NOVELS

Tivolem
Victor Rangel-Ribeiro
Pp 354. HB Rs 495 (1998)

Kirkus Reviews said of this book: "Longtime US resident Rangel-Ribeiro, a native of Goa who turned to fiction at age 72, debuts with a tale that luminously evokes life in that former Portuguese colony in India. The pace of this Narayan-like novel is sweetly contemplative, as befits the doings in the small backwater village of Tivolem, where everybody's business is everybody's business."

Set in the Goa of 1933 (and against the backdrop of momentous happenings, like Hitler and Gandhi's ascent in the news, and the Great Depression in the US), this book's focus is the village life of Goa of those times.

Marie-Santana returns home from Mozambique, leading to rumours in the village: she's rich, she had an abortion, and she possesses the evil eye. Violinist and former bureaucrat Simon is also back home, and the next-door neighbour of Marie-Santana. Their paths cross, and how.

Incidentally, this book won the 1998 Milkweed National Fiction Prize. Rangel-Ribeiro is known to be a writer meticulous over his art of writing; his stories are often strongly Goa-linked. His background in journalism, editing, creative writing and other fields makes him uniquely suited to tell the story, and tell it well.

In recent years, he has been taking pains to mentor young writers during his annual visits to Goa, and also via cyberspace. His initiatives have also led to the successful formation of groups like the GoaWriters' network[1].

The General Is Up *
Peter Nazareth
Writers Workshop, Calcutta.
Pp 187. Rs 80 (1984)

"This novel is a work of the imagination, not a historical, biographical or journalistic record of facts, personalities or events." Yet, Damibia looks like the Uganda of the early 1970s. The Goan community in that imaginary African country gets subsumed by expulsions much like Goans who faced Idi Amin.

A very readable novel, set in the expat Catholic Goan world. It is available currently through its Kolkata-based publishers, the Writers Workshop.

Peter Nazareth was himself born in Uganda (in 1940) and has been a major critic and writer of fiction and drama. He left Uganda as a senior finance officer, during the Idi Amin regime, and accepted a fellowship at Yale University. His other books include *In a Brown Mantle, Literature and Society*

---

[1] http://groups.yahoo.com/group/goawriters

in *Modern Africa, The Third World Writer (His Social Responsibility)* and *Two Radio Plays*. He has long been at the University of Iowa.

Nazareth attracted major media attention for teaching that university's popular course "Elvis as Anthology," which explores the deep mythological roots of Elvis Presley's role in popular culture. Other anthologies Nazareth edited include: *Uganda South Asians Exodus* (2002); *Critical Essays on Ngugi wa Thiong'o* (2000); *Goan Literature: A Modern Reader* (1983); *African Writing Today* (1981).

Boarding Party: The Last Action of the Calcutta Light Horse *
James Leasor
Allied Publishers, Bombay.
Pp 204. Rs 30 (1978)

Not exclusively Goa-related, though much of the action takes place here. It is World War II, and Allied ships are being decimated by German U-boats in the Indian Ocean. Apparently, information is being conveyed by a transmitter on one of three German ships in the neutral Portuguese harbour of Goa. Or so goes the British version of this dramatic story. In its pages we are told of how the German ships were sunk in an unusual action. The book was later adapted into a film called *The Sea Wolves*, largely shot in Goa. Author Leasor says this is a true story, but with changed or omitted names, and altered physical characteristics. Foreword by Admiral of the Fleet, Lord Mountbatten of Burma.

The Mango and the Tamarind Tree *
Leslie de Noronha
Writers Workshop, Calcutta.
Pp 236 (1970)

Not a political or historical story, neither a love story, says the author. He conceived of the idea and planned it in 1958, while in New York.

And he adds: "Then, on December 18th, 1961, the Indian militia entered Goa and, after 36 hours that electrified the world, the mighty Portuguese Empire came crashing down with the maximum of drama possible. And I found myself with the MS [manuscript] of what was overnight virtually a historical novel."

Peter Nazareth, who wrote a review of *The Dew Drop Inn* which was published in *World Literature Today*, says: "It is a sequel to *The Mango and the Tamarind Tree*: Raoul in the first novel gives up his lover (born in Kenya of a caste lower than his) because of pressure by his mother. In the sequel, Raoul regrets having given her up and he has now become gay — there are explicit descriptions of the gay scene in Bombay. He dies, near the end, in a plane crash.

"After Joseph Henry's evaluation published in the issue of *JSAL (Journal of South Asian Literature)*, Leslie wrote to Joe to say that Raoul's story was his own story. I know that Leslie died some years ago but I don't remember what year and what the cause of his death was."

Sorrowing Lies My Land
By Lambert Mascarenhas
Pp 213. Rs 175. (1999)

Former journalist and writer Ben Antao describes this novel thus: "*Sorrowing...* covers the time-span from roughly 1910 to about 1950. It is a political novel whose message is that the people of Goa under Portuguese rule were denied basic civil rights such as freedom of speech and assembly, and those who protested were quickly punished or imprisoned."

Antao notes that the first part of the action covers the period when Portugal was a republic before Salazar came into power and life in Goa was reasonably tolerable.

"The story revolves around Tobias, a *bhatkar* (landlord), and his family of nine. Tobias is unlike other *bhatkars* in that he loves to work in his fields. The story is narrated from the point of view of his youngest son Babush, who is six at the beginning of the story. The setting is not specifically stated but is close to Margao...."

One also comes across Colva, village life, post-1926 Goa (after the Colonial Act and Salazar), the campaign for civil rights, 1946 and the campaign by Indian socialist Rammanohar Lohia. His later work includes the play, *The Greater Tragedy*. In his 90s, Mascarenhas has also authored another novel in 2009, *Heartbreak Passage*.

Skin
Margaret Mascarenhas
New Delhi: Penguin Books India
Pp 257. Rs 250 (2001)
ISBN 0-14-100465-7 9780141004655

A diasporic novel, published by Penguin India, and then in translations in French (2002) and Portuguese (2006). The author is a columnist, novelist and consulting editor. She's an American citizen of Goan origin who grew up in Venezuela, and currently divides her time between Goa and California. Her other novels (to be published) include *Passion Fruit*, now renamed *The Disappearance of Irene Dos Santos*, and The French Club (working title). mmascgoa.tripod.com is where you can find the author's site online.

Mangoes and Chappaties *
Margaret Robert Drucker
NY: Vantage Press
Pp 256. $14.95 (1999)
ISBN 0-533-12870-6

"Examines the historical/political context and transitions with Portuguese and British India, beginning in 1927. Within this political context and the ensuing struggle for Indian independence, lives the De Albuquerque family. Through this family, the old belief system is challenged with a new school of belief and the advent of a new century. Desire for upward mobility forces many to confront the tradition of the caste system and their steadfast attachment to one's homeland. Through this remarkable book, one sees that success and wealth are achieved but at a demanding price. And through it all, the human spirit prevails."

Elsa's Joint and some Goan Characters
Remigio Botelho
Pp 205. Rs 150 (2002)
ISBN 81-7167-647-2

"A delightful novel about the petty troubles and travails that mark the lives of its residents... It all begins when Mr Fernandes loses his German-made umbrella in a church, where he goes to give a lecture on Panjim's history. Elsa's Joint, the tavern where all and sundry get together, bears witness to all...." The author, who passed away in 2001, was active in the media in Goa too.

The Girl
Sonia Faleiro
Viking.
Pp 128. HB. Rs 250 (2006)
ISBN 9780143063445

A quote from *The Hindustan Times*: "*The Girl*, published by Penguin, was set in a dazzlingly different Goa, safe from the trespassing eyes of tourists in a tiny village by the sea. The village's name, Azul, the Portuguese name for blue, could be evocative of azure seas and balmy beaches, but instead, very quickly, the reader finds himself in a Village of the Dead, where there is a Sad Café and an unnamed protagonist called the Girl, whose life is a vortex of loneliness."

The author is a journalist and writer.

She was born in Goa, and has lived in New Delhi and Edinburgh, and now works out of Mumbai. *The Girl* is her first novel.

Penance
Ben Antao
Pp 334. Rs 200 (2006)

A novel about relationships – one a conventional marriage, the other a same sex partnership – that went wrong.

Fellow-novelist Silviano C. Barbosa, also Canada-based and author of *The Sixth Night*, comments: "Author Ben Antao has succeeded in his first foray into a mainstream Canadian novel. The fact that Ben has based this novel on a more than familiar Catholic way of life and the fact that he is married to his Canadian-born wife and also the fact that he worked as a professional high school teacher in Toronto, has all worked very well for him in his portrayal of the Canadian Catholic teachers' intricate way of life in this Canadian novel. As a result the ethnic novelist leaves no stone unturned in making it a full fledged Canadian novel, and not an ethnic one."

Barbosa adds: "The first part of the novel follows the pattern indicated on the book's blurb, as the author uncovers the background of his characters with his typical show-and-tell craft, which most modern novelists adhere to. The second part is a lot more interesting and as the novel comes almost to an unexpected end, it holds the reader's undivided attention so much so that you can't possibly put the book down as the tragic end just bowls you over." Lino Leitão, another Canadian writer of Goan origin, has an insightful review at http://tinyurl.com/cbqyjj

Blood & Nemesis
Ben Antao
Panjim: Goan Observer
Pp 318. Rs 250. CN$25. (2005)

Blood & Nemesis was released on June 18, 2005, in Goa by

freedom fighter-author James Fernandes. UK-based expat Dr. Cornel da Costa says in a review: "In this very absorbing story, we note the ever-vigilant police presence represented by Jovino Colaço and his immediate boss Gaspar Dias. Both are determined to suppress any Goan anti-Portuguese sentiments and political activity sympathetic to Indian nationalism.

"They take it upon themselves, on behalf of the authoritarian Portuguese administration, to bait freedom fighters, capture them, physically abuse them and then incarcerate them in the infamous Aguada jail in Goa. Their particular quarry from May 1955 was a fellow Goan, Santan Barreto.

"They kept a close eye on him and on his friends who usually spent their leisure time at Bombay Cafe in the town centre of Margao in south Goa. This cat and mouse strategy is captured brilliantly in the novel. It depicts Jovino, the policeman ... on his motorbike, as a power-hungry individual, with a weakness for drink, gambling and prostitutes...."

Antao's other novels include *Living on the Market* (Palabras-Press, Calgary, 2008), *The Priest And His Karma* (May 2009), and *The Tailor's Daughter*.

The Brahmans *
Francisco Luis Gomes (1829-1869)
Published by the Dr Francis Luis Gomes Centenary Committee
Mumbai: Sindhu Publications
Pp 185. Rs 10 (1969?)

This book is made up of two parts, containing 21 and 17 chapters. Plus a letter to the French writer, poet and politician Lamartine.

The author says: "The germ of the novel is a historical fact. I have developed it, depicting the manners of the Anglo-Indian society, and creating a few characters and episodes, less from a creative impulse than by the compulsion exerted by the meagerness of the theme."

Litterateur Armando Menezes says in the book's introduction: "It is, frankly, journalism in disguise.... The feeling of superiority that comes of pride in caste or race is embodied in Magnod (Magnum odium?), a Hindu Brahmin, and in Robert Davis, an Irish tobacco-planter at Oudh. The dramatic conflict in the novel is the clash of two Brahmanisms – the brown and the white."

The Gift of the Holy Cross *
Lino Leitão
Peepal Tree, Leeds
Pp 184. UKP 6.99 (1999)
ISBN 1 900715 15 7

From colonial Goa – and its hybrid of Portuguese Catholicism and the Hindu caste system – this novel has the scent of Salcete (the author was born in Varca, and is set in Cavelossim and Carmona).

It suggests the real gainers of the end of Portuguese rule in 1961 were a new commercial elite, while the local culture gets eroded. Mario Jaques is the central character through whom this story is narrated.

Leitao has acknowledged the historical incidents and personalities alluded to in the text, but asserted that this is "not a historical novel". Completed in 1983, it was published only in 1997. Goa-born Leitão lived in Uganda and then in Canada, where he passed away recently.

A Kind of Absence *
João da Veiga Coutinho
Stamford CT: Yuganta Press
Pp 127. Rs 250 $9.95 US (1997)
ISBN 0-938999-10-9

Critic Peter Nazareth has this to say of the book, writing in 1998: "*A Kind of Absence* reopens history on the 500th anniversary of the voyage by Vasco da Gama which paved the way for the colonization of Goa and the consequential displacement of a people....

"Coutinho's work reads like a novel with the narrator holding conversations with dead historians, with himself, and with the poet Camoens, who says, 'And like the Greeks, Goans also believe that something great has happened on their exiguous soil, though they are hard put to say exactly what it is.' Every myth vanishes when questioned."

Check historian Dr Teotonio R de Souza's[2] polemical review of this book.

The Dew Drop Inn
Leslie de Noronha
Writers Workshop, Calcutta
Pp 297. Rs 250 HB. Rs 50 FB (1994)
ISBN 81-7189-730-4(HB) 81-7189-731-2 (FB)

The author was a doctor in England. He believes in the advice he once received there: that a trivial incident can change a life. This happens in the book too.

Shantimarg is a fictitious montage of "all Himalayan hill stations". Medical colleges at Bombay and London get featured here too. This book, in part is, "to a great extent autobiographical, if highly dramatized". *The Mango and the Tamarind Tree* was Noronha's earlier novel.

Touched by the Toe
Alexandre Moniz Barbosa
Palavra Publications, Panjim
Pp 212 Rs 150 (2004)
Set in the mid-sixteenth century. Describes itself as "a fictional tale surrounding the religious hysteria that erupted in Goa on the arrival of the body of St Francis Xavier."

---

[2]http://tinyurl.com/7wvqnp

Karmelin
Damodar Mauzo
Translated by Vidya Pai
New Delhi: Sahitya Akademi
Pp 281. Rs 125 (2004)
ISBN 81-260-1918-2

    A young Goan Catholic girl is orphaned, and fights against poverty. The story tracks the fortunes of Karmelin, who is let down by her drunk-husband and pursued by poverty. She migrates to Kuwait. A story of sexual exploitation, caste conflict, Arab bosses, and modern day Kuwait and Goa.

Acchev (The Upheaval)
Pundalik Naik
Translated by Vidya Pai
Pp 144. HB Rs 295 (2002)

    First published in 1977, but only recently made visible to the non-Devanagari Konkani reader, following a translation. Focuses on peasant life in Ponda district, with the backdrop of industrialisation and mining.

    Maria Aurora Couto writes: "Pundalik Naik's *Acchev* is one of the glories of Goan literature. Written in Konkani, it deserved a wider readership which English could give.... his theme of the destruction of Goa's exceptional environment by mining had a resonance that would be appreciated both in India and abroad."

On A Goan Beach *
Remigio Botelho
Pp 181. Rs 90. US$3 (1994)

    An expat Indian returns to his roots and finds his seaside village of Anjuna has grown into a hippy paradise. This is a story of drug-taking, peddlers, traffickers and love. The other works by the same author include *Destination Goa*, and *Goa of the Gods*.

The Sixth Night
Silviano C. Barbosa
Toronto: Goa Raj Books
Pp 314 HB Np (2004)
ISBN 0-973620-00-5

Canada-based expat Barbosa (b. 1949) writes this novel about a Catholic girl growing up in the 1950s. It is also about caste discrimination of the time (not that it's all vanished now), falling in love with a foreigner, personal loss flowing out of the 1961 Indo-Portuguese conflict....

This book describes itself as "a story of love, hate, jealousy and intrigue [offering] great insights into Goan life, traditions, and customs." *The Sixth Night* in the title of the book refers to one such tradition itself.

Tales from the Attic
By Savia Viegas
Goa: Saxtti Foundation
Pp 130 Rs 200 (2007)
ISBN 81-85569-74-6

Janhavi Acharekar describes it thus in *The Hindu*'s Literary Review: "A dark and brooding narrative about the inner workings of a state generally associated with its intoxicating air and carefree residents, Savia Viegas' debut novel takes you to the post-Liberation era in Goa – a time well before the hippy, the tourist and the budget airline eras that transformed the state into beach bacchanalia.

"A self-published work, this is the latest among dark writings set in the sunny state (Sonia Faleiro's *The Girl* is another such work). It is the story of Marri, a schoolteacher who drifts into the nooks and crannies of her past under the influence of anesthesia.... *Tales from the Attic* is really a collection of stories within a broader narrative, as Marri turns *sutradhar*, narrating tales of other characters even as she records her own experiences.

"The novel is therefore largely about her interaction with the others – the Gaudda woman from across the border in Karnataka, the labourers willing to live in bondage in exchange for food and shelter and their son Khoniji, later baptised Jose, who sexually abuses her well into adolescence in the attic. Eventually, Marri finds herself in Bombay during the textile era, straddling a failed marriage in a big city even as she keeps alive her connection with her rural past."

The Tailor's Daughter
Ben Antao
Panjim: Goan Observer
Pp 334 HB Rs 300 (2007)
ISBN 81-89837-03-6

This is the third of journalist-educator-writer Ben Antao's novels, after *Blood & Nemesis* and *Penance*. Comments a review published on the academyx.wordpress.com blog: "I found *The Tailor's Daughter* remarkable not for its descriptions of casteism in India (which was poorly done) but rather for its vivid descriptions of intimate scenes, something that is rare in Goan books."

Viva Santiago
Colin Fernandes
Penguin Books
Pp 137 Rs 199 (2008)
ISBN 9780-14-310398-1

Promises the "sights, sounds and flavours of Goa, and a good dose of sex, drugs and rock music." The author, born in 1979 and based in New Delhi, has also been a journalist.

DNA said in a review: "Colin Fernandes' novel, *Viva Santiago*, shifts back and forth in time to tell the story of the doobie-rolling-Mojito-sipping Santiago Alvarez and his grandson Alonso Gonzalez. Set mainly in Goa, the breezy narrative marries Goa's past and present. It describes a Goa that was made up of small islands that you had to take boats to cross, as well as present day Goa, rave parties et al., where a rented bike can take you from North to South in less than a few hours.

"The narrative hinges on an exciting treasure hunt across famous locations in Goa, with the clues hidden in the lyrics of Bob Dylan songs. How many clues must a man have to solve, before he finds some treasure? Alonso Gonzalez unwillingly finds out."

"Fernandes writes with the expertise of a seasoned pot-smoker, throwing in detailed accounts of Santiago's joint-rolling and chillum-loading processes. From the artwork on the cover to the anecdotes inside, *Viva Santiago* is interspersed with a large dose of revelries that lace the adventurous trail. Many locations in the book are actual places which one can still visit in Goa, such as the Shiva rock-face at Vagator Beach and St. George Lighthouse at Ilha Grão (Grande Island). Like a *Da Vinci Code* for stoners and rock music lovers, this novel is a thriller with jokes and interesting trivia about growing up in the land called Goa."

The Hedonist Empire
Arun Sinha
New Delhi: Peacock Books
Printed by Maureen Printers, Goa.
Pp 251. Rs 150 (1996)
ISBN 81-7525-018-6

By *The Navhind Times*' long-time editor. "Chetan Rambol, a North Indian Brahmin in his thirties, runs away from his despotic father's village home in pursuit of happiness to Goa Portuguesa, which has been described to him by many as the most ideal country for sinners."

Monsoon *
A novelization by Randor Guy of Jag Mundhra's film "Monsoon".
Magna Books.
Pp 122. Rs 75 (1997)

"Erotic Goa" is the backdrop and stereotyped Goa is the setting of a film starring Helen Brodie, Gulshan Grover and others. It packages itself as "an unusual story of love, adultery and rebirth".

An IITian, Calcutta-born film-maker Mundhra has done his thesis on motion pictures – comparing the marketing practices in Hollywood and Bollywood. Since 1979, he has become a full-time film-maker. He is also known for his string of horror and erotic thrillers.

Gates of Fire *
Elwyn Chamberlain
Fontana/Collins
Pp 410. UKP 3.95 (1978)

Mysticism of the East, violence, sex, drugs ... a large part of it set in Goa. If you believe life imitates art, check it out here. Subsequent events in Goa seem to be following what Chamberlain depicted in his 'fiction'. This novel talks about corrupt officials, policemen mixing with the mafia, and the sleezy side of tourism.

Govind
H. Ratnakar Rau
Disha Books, Orient Longman: Bombay
Pp 302. Pb Rs 170 (1996)
ISBN 81 250 0801 2

This book is set in colonial times. It's Karnataka-born author Rau (1914-1995) studied in Bombay, and then had to leave his studies to look after his family rice and oil mill in Goa. For five-and-half decades, Rau ran businesses in different towns in Goa – in fields as varied as rice, oil and flour milling, ice-making, electric supply, farming, poultry keeping and selling machinery and electric appliances. While doing so, he wrote in English, Marathi and Konkani.

Then journalist (and later Director of Information) Rajesh Singh, reviewing the book in *The Navhind Times* comments: "Govind is the veteran Marathi writer H. Ratnakar Rau's first novel in English. It is the story of a Goan Hindu orphan, who, born when the State was in the grip of (the) Inquisition, journeys to manhood with the help of a captain in the Portuguese army who prevents his baptism to Christianity. In a way, thus, it is also the story of Dom Pedro, the captain who risks death in defying the law that all orphans have to be necessarily baptised. The manoeuvres that he adopts towards this end makes for fascinating reading."

Angela's Goan Identity
Carmo D'Souza
Self-published
Pp 147 Rs 35 (1994)

Writes editor Ashwin Tombat: "'Goan identity' means so many different things to so many people, that the term is commonly used and abused, no two writers or two readers will quite be able to agree on what it connotes exactly."

This is a story of a Goan *bhatkar* (landlord) family from around Calangute, a former beach village that has been drastically changed by the impact of tourism.

D'Souza makes his point well enough to be appreciated by critics like Peter Nazareth. See also the comments of Donna Young on this work, earlier on in this book. Carmo D'Souza's other work includes *Jose's Dreams: A New World Order* (Pp 110, Rs 150, 2008).

Jacob & Dulce: Sketches from Indo-Portuguese Life
Gip (Francisco João da Costa)
Translated by Alvaro Noronha da Costa
Sahitya Akademi, New Delhi

Pp 196 Rs 115 (2004)
Portuguese edition first published in 1896.
ISBN 81-260-1968-9

When this book surfaced in a reasonably-priced English edition not long back, it quickly gained its fans in contemporary Goa. The book comprises the author's nineteenth century word sketches that critique Goan Christian society and the government of the time. Gip used a few place names that coincided with some in Margão, and it was assumed that the town of Breda was Margão itself and that the characters described belonged to well-known families of that town.

- Other related works with a Goa connection include Richard Zimler's *Guardian of the Dawn*, set again amidst the Inquisition (Constable, Pp 371, 2005); the post-1961 set of two plays in English called *Goa and Abbe Faria* by Asif Currimbhoy (pp 195); Sushila Fonseca's *The Secret of the Diamond Ring* (Pauline Publications, Rs 60, Pp 192, 2007); *The Red-Headed Shrew* by Melanie Ruth (Daughters of St Paul, Rs 7.50, 1986); Frank Simoes' *Goa* (Roli Books, Rs 295, 2004); and Tony D'Souza's more recent *The Konkans*, which is charmingly narrated but with a story-line that sometimes seems to get its facts wrong (Rupa, Pp 282, Rs 295, 2008). *Stephanie* by Winston Graham came via the Reader's Digest Condensed Books (London, 1993), at a time just when Goa was becoming a fashionable tourist destination in that part of the globe. Paul Mann's *Ganja Coast* (a George Sansi Mystery) is a bizarre story about the drug mafia in Goa. Mind you, it was written long before the mainstream media started repeatedly writing about real and imagined drugs-politics-tourism connections in Goa. Life imitating art? Not easily found in Goa, but new and second-hand copies are available via Amazon.com. *Once Upon A Time In Aparanta* is by journalist-turned-writer Sudeep Chakravarti. A description: "The tale of Dino Dantas, protestor and self-appointed guardian of Aparanta, and his innkeeper cousin Antonio begins here, in the sleepy village of Socorro Do Mundo by the Sea, where time holds little meaning and the haze of nostalgia is as binding a force as faith in the benevolence of Our Lady of Perpetual Succour...."

MEMOIRS, ESSAYS

Goa: A Daughter's Story
Maria Aurora Couto
Pp 436. Rs 350 (2004)

This widely-noticed book on Goa has been called a "unique blend of biography, memoir and social history" by the Other India Bookstore. Robert Newman wrote in an Amazon.com review: "I liked Couto's book because it emphasized the synthesis of Hindu and Catholic tradition within Goa's culture, a synthesis that is under strong attack by rightwing communalist forces today. Whether or not that tradition will survive remains to be seen. She also worries, rightly, about the effects of mass tourism on the culture and ecology of her beloved Goa."

Says Couto: "It has appealed to a wide cross-section of readers outside Goa, including a few scholars from Portugal and Brasil who have found their way to Aldona clutching the book. That is my reward and it is best to ignore the mutterings within Goa that refer to caste and elitism."

Glad Seasons in Goa
Frank Simoes
Viking/Penguin
Pp 316. HB Rs 295 (1994)

"[M]uch more than a memoir or an entertaining travelogue.... it is an unforgettable portrait of a people and an irresistible way of life." Ad professional Frank Simoes' story of his return to Goa, and more.

Goa and the Continent of Circe *
Robert de Souza
Wilco, Bombay
Pp 215. Rs 12.50 (1973)

This is an advocate and judge's response to Nirad Chaudhuri's 'Continent of Circe', and particularly his characterization of Goans there.

Khushwant Singh, writes in the Foreword: "Nirad C. Chaudhuri's remarks on the Goans being half-caste meztizos who supply Bombay's cooks, waiters, fiddlers, maid-servants and bordellos is to be taken in the same way as his opinions on other subjects.

"Nirad has great affection for the Goans as he has for all go-ahead robust people. He has adopted a young Goan boy living next door as his own and throws a birthday party for the child every year.

"He is devoted to the boy's mother. But none of that will stop him from poking fun at her half-European dress, curried pizzas and chi-chi *Hobson Jobson*. That is Nirad Chaudhuri – the prickly pear with thorns outside to screw the flesh and succulent juicy friendship within."

Man from the Sun: The Story of the Kosambis
Indrayani Sawkar
Popular Prakashan, Mumbai
Pp 225, Rs 225 (2001)

This is the story of Dharmanand Kosambi, a biographical novel written by his grand-daughter, about the "scholar and philosopher who had the courage to transcend middle class notions regarding family and occupation and contained the irrepressible desire to move towards an existence that would reach philosophical heights." A very insightful read indeed.

Censored Courtship
Dr Jose Francisco Martins
Pp 560. Rs 675 (2000)

The author, who died recently, was a freedom fighter. This book comprises the correspondence between him and his fiancee (and wife-to-be) in Portuguese colonial times, when he was jailed at Aguada

Goa and the Blue Mountains or Six Months of Sick Leave
Richard F. Burton
Pp 368 HB Rs 365 (1991)

Wikipedia, the online volunteer-crafted encyclopaedia, describes Captain Sir Richard Francis Burton KCMG FRGS (1821-1890) as "an English explorer, translator, writer, soldier, Orientalist, ethnologist, linguist, poet, hypnotist, fencer and diplomat."

He explored Asia and Africa, and had an extraordinary knowledge of languages and cultures. Believed to have spoken 29 European, Asian, and African languages, Burton is best known for discovering the source of the Nile.

These pages contain impressions of Goa, Malabar, Calicut and the Nilgiris. Tune in to Burton's tone: "That Panjim is a Christian town appears instantly from the multitude and variety of the filthy feeding hogs that infest the streets. The pig here occupies the social position that he does in Ireland, only he is never eaten when his sucking days are past.

"Panjim loses much by close inspection. The streets are dusty and dirty, of a most disagreeable brick colour, and where they are paved, the pavement is old and bad.

"The doors and window-frames of almost all the houses are painted green, and none but the richest admit light through anything more civilized than oyster-shells. The balcony is a prominent feature, but it presents none of the gay scenes for which it is famous in Italy and Spain."

Anthropologist Robert S. Newman, an avid book reviewer who has a few hundred reviews on Amazon.com, has a sharply critical review of the work, on Amazon.com

He writes: "Burton wrote what could have been a very interesting book, never mind accuracy. But his sneering, racist attitudes of contempt for everyone and everything, his total willingness to enforce his will on Indians with kicks and punches, his constant professions of boredom, and his scorn for each person he meets, even his own countrymen, cover the travel with a disgusting sauce, even though he may have been typical of his times (and one should not condemn, blah, blah, blah)"

This is a copyright-expired book, now getting reprinted in India. Its full-text is also available online[3].

From Goa to Patagonia
Alfredo B. de Mello
Broadway Book Centre, Panjim.
Pp 215, Rs 295 (2007)
ISBN 978-81-905716-1-6

The author is the son of a prominent Goan doctor Dr. Froilano de Mello (ex-director of erstwhile Escola Médica de Goa, doctor and scientist), and his memoirs tell us of the times past. Following Mello on his trip half-way round the world, into business, and many adventures along the way, one gets a feel of life in colonial Goa – from the eyes of a priviledged member of society then.

> ■ Among the other memoirs, autobiographies and biographies are Aloysius Soares' two-volumed *Down The Corridors of Time* (published in the early 1970s in Bombay, now out of print); Mervyn Maciel's interesting account of his life and times in colonial Africa titled *Bwana Karani (ISBN 0-86303-261-3);* and Shashikar

[3] http://www.wollamshram.ca/1001/Goa/Goa.htm

Kelekar's biography of *Telo de Mascarenhas* (Government of India's Ministry of Information and Broadcasting, in its Builders of Modern India series).

- Ivan Arthur's *Once More Upon A Time* is a biography of businessman-industrialist Pascoal Menezes of the Cosme Matias Menezes group. For private circulation; publication details are not mentioned. *In Search of Self-Fulfilment* is freedom fighter José Francisco Martins' life-story (Rajhauns Vitaran, 1997, ISBN 81-85854-79-3). *My Goa* is politician Luizinho Faleiro's well-written autobiography, obviously penned with professional assistance and published in 1999.

- See also *In Search of Tomorrow* (Edila Gaitonde, Allied, 1987, Rs 60); *The Story of My Life by Dom Peres* (175 pp) and *How Long is Forever* (Pp 186, 2006, Rs 250), the autobiography of radio announcer Imelda Dias (Tavora), who recently wrote a sequel.

IN VERSE

Selected Poems: Joseph Furtado 1872-1947 *
Published by Philip Furtado, Bombay
Sankli Street, Byculla, Bombay

Joseph Furtado is the author of *A Goan Fiddler*, and a prominent early Goan poet writing in English. His son Philip Furtado explains, in the foreword, that the work was "first published in 1942 and limited to a hundred copies intended for private circulation and distribution to certain libraries. No copies were sent for review or offered for sale."

Of 125 poems, the earliest ('The Italian Architect') was composed in 1903 and the latest, 'Kismet', in 1939. Sections of this book include: 'De Profundis', 'Childhood Poems', 'Nature Poems', 'Love Poems', 'Humorous Poems', 'Poems to My Motherland', and 'Portuguese Poems'.

Reviewer Augusto Pinto says[4] of Joseph Furtado: "For a man to whom it was not even a second but a third language, Furtado had a remarkable ear for the sounds of English. In this he is unlike most Indian poets, who prefer to work with images; and only a Sarojini Naidu can come close to match him in this respect."

And: "Keki N. Daruwalla in his 'Introduction' to the influential anthology of Indian English poetry, *Ten Twentieth Century Indian Poets*, points out that Furtado was the first to see the potential of using 'Indian' English in poetry."

Goan Poetry *
Compiled by R. V. Pandit.
Bhagwati Prakashan, Goa.
Pp 73. Rs 15 (1976)

A two-volume anthology of verse by Goan poets who were living at the time of publication.

Book One (covering Portuguese, English and Marathi) includes the work of Vincente Correia-Afonso, Hermogenes Furtado, Philip Furtado, Furtunato De Melo, George Menezes, Prof Armando Menezes, Dileep S. Phaldesai, Dr Jose Rangel, Mario Rodrigues, Aniceto Rodrigues, Manuel C Rodrigues, Augusto De Rozario Rodrigues, Dr Bailon De Sa, Manuel De Souza, Cyrano Valles, and B.B. Borkar.

Book Two (covering Konkani) includes Bayabhav, Shankar Bhandari, Pandurang Bhangi, Narayan Desai, Gajanan Jog, Pundalik Nayak, Shankar Ramani, Madhavi Sardesai, Dr ManoharRai Sardesai, Vijaya V. Sarmalkar, N. Shivdas and Dr R. V. Pandit.

The 1917-born compiler was a photographer attached to Mahatma Gandhi's party, and a publisher who brought out works of poetry in Goa. As an aside, it might seem odd today to note that this was an Emergency-time book, pub-

---

[4]http://www.mail-archive.com/goanet-news@lists.goanet.org/msg01352.html

lished on Indira Gandhi's birthday, and "respectfully dedicated" to "the resolute leader of a firm united nation".

At the time this text was published, Pandit himself already had ten other collections of poems some of which had been translated by Thomas Gay. Of these, seven were originally in the Devanagari, and three in the Roman script. There were also four on folk tales (Devanagari), and translations in Hindi and Kannada (one each) and in Marathi (two, translations of stories by him into that language).

An Anthology of Modern Konkani Poems: Book I *
Dr Manohar Sardessai (Ed.)
Gomant Bharati, Borkar Printers, Margao
Pp 75. (1964)

Konkani poems with free English rendering. 'Kaka' Acharya Kalelkar, in the foreword, compares the (then) position of Konkani to the language of Assam, or Asamia. His foreword is titled, "The Spring Time For Konkani".

My Song, Ma Chanson, O Meu Canto
ManoharRai Sardesai
New Age, Verna
Pp 180 HB Rs 250 (2008)
ISBN 81-906385-0-5

A collection of the Sorbonne-educated ManoharRai Sardesai's poems in three languages – Konkani, English and French. Edited and compiled by the late Jorge de Abreu Noronha.

Included here is his paean to the Goan diaspora 'We Are The World Wanderers' and a Portuguese-language version of his 'Otthra Jun' or The 18th of June, the day that marks the launch of the movement in the mid-1940s for the last surge to oppose Portuguese rule. Sardesai's themes consistently explore the Goan reality.

Jaime de Mello and Samir Kelekar, in an online post

via Goanet[5], offer a translation of The 18th of June, which gives a hint of the rousing nature of Sardesai's verse. Sardesai's name has also been rendered as Sardessai and Manohar Sardesai (instead of ManoharRai) in some texts.

Last Bus to Vasco
Brian Mendonça, self-published.
Pp 70 HB, with CD. Rs 150 (2007)

Fifty poems on Goa are included in this book. Featured are poems titled after Souza Lobo (the restaurant at Calangute), Good Friday at Cuncolim, and Mapusa Memories. So, how local can one get? Interesting... Four useful pages of notes explaining the context, at the end.

This is publishing professional Brian Mendonça's 2006 self-published work, with an audio CD of his readings. Mendonça is an editor with a prominent book publishing firm in New Delhi. He has travelled across India, reading and promoting his work.

Tamarind Leaf *
R. V. Pandit. Translated by Thomas Gay.
Bhagwati Prakashan, Palem-de-Siridao, Goa Velha.
Rs 3 (1967)

Translator Gay writes: "As Shri Pandit's translator, I have been both charmed and attracted by the range and depth of his inspiration. He is by turns simple, profound, humorous, pathetic, witty, solemn, tender, sarcastic...."

A note on the Konkani language in the book says: "Often acclaimed as one of India's sweetest tongues, it is richly expressive and flexible and has absorbed many words and locutions from Tulu, Marathi, Canarese, Arabic, Portuguese, English and Persian."

---

[5] http://www.mail-archive.com/goanet@goanet.org/msg28024.html

Loads: A Book of Poems *
By Remo Fernandes.
Pp 48. Rs 25 (1980)

Pop-star, architect, social critic the young Remo Fernandes' angry (mostly) poems comprise this collection. Many of these poems were written while he was travelling in Europe and north Africa in the 1970s.

They end on the note of homecoming. (Incidentally, in 2008, Remo caused some heartburn by highlighting corruption issues in Goa, and pledging to leave the place!) "This book is dedicated to all Goans who have died frustrated. May there be no more."

This is a book which influenced us in our college days. Remo is still working on the music — one number released via Facebook in October 2009 — which continues to make people think. This self-published book is definitely unavailable and out-of-print.

I Exist: Poems by Santan Rodrigues
Writers Workshop, Calcutta
Pp 41. HB Rs 20 Flexiback Rs 10.

This book describes itself as "a first volume of verse". Published when the late Rodrigues was in his twenties, and he co-edited *Kavi*, a poetry quarterly. Rodrigues (1948-2006) died early, after working in the corporate world (and ruing the fact that he couldn't write more verse).

Dom Moraes: Collected Poems 1957-1987
Penguin
Rs 167. Rs 60 (1987)
ISBN 0-14-010340-6

This book's cover calls it "thirty years of poetry from India's greatest living English-language poet." This is a thumbnail description of the writer, in the Wikipedia: "Dominic Francis Moraes (19 July 1938–2 June 2004), popularly known as Dom Moraes was a Goan writer, poet and columnist. He published nearly 30 books."

This book includes four sections of poems. Much of the imagery focuses on places other than Goa. Not surprising, for Moraes was the son of editor and author Frank Moraes. With his father, he travelled through Sri Lanka, Australia, New Zealand, the "whole of South East Asia", and he also edited magazines in London, Hong Kong and New York.

Says the book, "He has visited every country in the world except Antarctica, which, he adds, is not a country."

Themes of the poems include Kanheri Caves, Sailing to England, French Lesson, From Tibet, Two From Israel, Kinshasa, and the like.

Heart Beat
Marinella Proenca
Pp 55. Rs 650 (2007)

Fifty-five pages of poems, printed on quality paper along with some really artistic photographs. A sigh for the Goa that was. heartbeatgoa.com

My Goa and Other Poems *
R. V. Pandit. Translated by Thomas Gay.
Rs 8. $2. Sh 15. (1971)

"In these 65 poems, Shri Pandit mirrors the many-sided life of 'his' Goa. As a Goan, he knows the tragic poverty that stalks beneath the waving palms, that lurks even in the *zamindar*'s stately mansion."

Star Dust: A collection of poems in English for children.
David Furtado
Candolim
Rs 125 (2007)

Some 25 poems set in Goa. Foreword by Tomazinho Cardozo. Colour illustrations by art college students.

The Dreaming House
Tanya Mendonsa
HarperCollins
Hb Rs 299 (2009)

This book is authored by a Goan who resettled in Moira village, and was just recently released (December 2009) when this compilation was going to press.

Mendonsa writes: "I had written poetry all my life, but in fits and starts; the longest creative periods being, of course, when I was unhappily in love. But from the first night in my old-new house, like a water source being unblocked, the words flowed onto paper as effortlessly as the sweet air I breathed."

The book has been described thus: "Conceived of as a journey within a book, a journey in both geographical and spiritual terms, *The Dreaming House* is an anthology of poems in two parts. The first, titled 'The Voyage Out', is composed of poems on people the author has met – whether in real or imaginary life. The second, 'The Country Beyond', focuses ... on the natural world and its ability to change human beings."

The Day Before The Day After
Dom Martin
TransGalactic Publications, California.
Pp 85. US$4.95. 1985.
ISBN 0-9616078-0-7

This work comes from the US-based Goan surrealist artist, and is dedicated to "the few whose solar wills can prevent humanity's eclipse". It was penned at a time when a nuclear disaster was seen as more likely than our currently perceived global perils, such as global warming.

It contains two parts, 'The Day Before' and 'The Day After'. For a profile of the artist and articles written by him see http://www.dommartin.us

Fruits of My Labour *
Jonas Correia, Carona
Pp 37. Rs 100 (1974)

A locally-focussed book, written by a resident of Aldona village, in Bardez, North Goa. It even includes a poem to Carona, and another to Aldona.

■ Other works in verse include *Eve's Revenge: Stories of Nemesis* (by Ethel da Costa, Broadway, 2008); *Borrowed Time* (Manohar Shetty, Praxis, 1988); *Goan Vignettes and Other Poems* (Ashok Mahajan, Oxford University Press, 1986); *A Rainbow & A Star* (by the late Tithi Tavora who tragically lost her life, Writers Workshop, 2002); *Destino Poemas* (Judit Beatriz de Souza, Imprensa Nacional Goa, 1955); *Dream Flower* (Dr Bicaji Ganecar, Green Stars Publications, 2000); *A Brutal Sunset* and *The Ten Commandments* (both by Bob D'Costa, Writers Workshop, 1982 and 1985 respectively); *Asylum* (Jerry Pinto, Allied Publishers, 2003); *Down The Arches of the Years* (Bailon de Sa, 1995); *Night Chasers and Other Poems* (Roy Albuquerque); and *Poems* (Leslie de Noronha, Writers Workshop, 1965).

LEGENDS, FOLK TALES, PROVERBS

Legends of Goa
Mario Cabral e Sa
India Book House
Pp 119. HB Rs 395 (1998)

Historical legends of Goa. Stories of Mogrem, Kushtoba, Navadurga, the crocodiles of the Mandovi, and the Orlem Ghor (big house) live on in these pages.

Says this book, "Legends are, however, not merely tall tales but reflect in them the realities of the past from the very creation of Goa to the advent and departure of colonial rule." Illustrated by Mario Miranda. "Presented" by the Goa Tourism Department.

Legends of the Konkan
Arthur Crawford
Pp 300. HB Rs 265 (1987)

First published in 1909. Dedicated "by special permission" to the Maharajah Gaekwar (sic) of Baroda.

Written by an author who spent two decades in the Southern Konkan as assistant collector. Some stories have a bearing on Goa. For instance, Chapter V is 'How Parashuram cursed the Konkan'.

Konkani Folk Tales
Retold by Olivinho J. F. Gomes
National Book Trust, India.
Pp 232. Rs 75 (2007)
ISBN 978-81-237-5083-5

This anthology calls itself "at times wacky, at times full of whimsy and at other times serious." Twenty stories, plus an introduction, from an official turned academic who rose to become the acting vice chancellor of Goa University before passing away in 2009.

Themes of the folk tales include parental and filial love, family happiness, adventures of children and adults, love and fear of the unknown, natural greed, and love of wealth and glamour, among other topics. Reasonably priced for its size, not surprising as it is published by the state-funded NBT.

Folk Tales of Goa *
Meurin
Bombay
Pp 61. Rs 2 (n.d.)

Stories like that of *Kolo-Koli* (the foxy couple), *Kolo-Manghem, Attulem Bittulem, Siumami*, and two Goan devil stories. Arthur Francis 'Meurin' Santos collected folk-tales as he travelled through life as a migrant Goan in Igatpuri, Jubbulpore (sic) and Bombay.

Goan Fairy Tales *
Selected by Claudiana de Noronha Ataide Lobo
Translated by Anselmo Rodrigues
Panjim, Goa : Tipografia Sadananda
Pp 79 (1964)

Stories have names like The King's Godson, The Cunning Fox, and The Goldsmith. The most-charming is perhaps the last, titled 'A Story Without End'.

Jorge de Graça Ataide Lobo, writing in December 1964, says his mother had asked him to compile these selected fairy tales into a book. And "... her main purpose and fear was that such a rich manifestation of our folklore might be lost for posterity...."

A Glance Through the Goan Folklore *
Robert de Souza
Casa Editora, Nova Goa
Pp 35 (1930)
Available in photocopy form for reference at Central Library's Rare Books Section.

A quote: "Goa is essentially a land of Muses. Camoes, Bocage, Tomas Ribeiro, Mrs Florencia de Morais, Dr Alberto O. de Castro, during their sojourn in the Edenic soil of Goa;

and Floriano Barreto, Paulino Dias, Nascimento de Mendonça, and others of our 'Land of Palm and Cashew Tree', have sung and sanctified her charms and glorified her name by leaving works of art that she can boast of as her own."

Robert de Souza says that political *podam* have become very conspicuous in Goa, especially in the province of Salcete – their main birth place. Of other kinds of Concani (as Konkani was then spelt) poetry, the most noteworthy is the satire.

Goan folk seem to be specially born for censure and criticism; and rightfully satire should be its legitimate language, the author comments.

Durpodam, or refrain-mandos, says this book, are a medley of disconnected ideas dressed in flowery wording. It looks at the origin of the mandos, besides the *zoti* (the labour song) and the *zagor*.

Says this book: "Specially in Karachi and in Bombay, Goan communities seem to travel much further in the artistic line, and slowly but surely we must expect also a gradual renaissance at home."

This book talks about suggestive riddles, truth-embodying proverbs and sayings, maxims and aphorisms, epigrams and parables, lays and legends, tales and myth. Some of the lore is of ancient Hindu origin.

Tales & Tellers of Goa *
V.S. Sukhtanker.
Pp 121, Rs 12.50 (1974)

Work from a Marathi short story-writer, and described by the author as a "new approach... to the presentation of folk-lore".

This book contains five stories across 58 pages, and also longer chapters on the music and songs of Goa.

Says Sukhtanker, "These stories should be considered... as vignettes of social life in Goa, as it fascinated me in my younger days in the nineteen-twenties." The introduction to the volume says, "Each one of these (five) sketches is a lovely setting for a folk-tale which is woven round a folk song."

Konkani Proverbs
V. P. Chavan
Pp 90 HB Rs 95 (1995)

For all Konkani lovers – picturesque, punchy, colloquial speech. Says author Rao Saheb Dr V.P. Chavan, LM&S, "Among Orientals, proverbs form the foundation of moral and political philosophy. They have a special influence in impressing upon the minds of the masses fundamental principles of morality and noble living." He says that Konkani proverbs "not only abound in certain figures of speech but they are impressive as well."

SHORT STORIES

The Harvest and other Short Stories from Goa
Manohar Shetty (Ed)
Institute Menezes Braganza, Panaji.
Pp 127, Pb Rs 50 (nd)

This is a modestly-published, reasonably priced but very interesting collection of short stories from Goa. For those of us who (rightly) complain about a lack of translations in Goan writing, here is one silver lining. Don't get mislead by the fact that this slim book's price is a mere fifty rupees.

It includes the writing of Mahabaleshwar Sail, Prakash Pariekar, Vasant Bhagwant Sawant, Shashank Sitaram, Ramnath Gajanan Gavde, Prasad Nilkanth Malkarnekar, Sheela Kolambkar, Meena Kakodkar, Manohar Hirba Sardessai, Vaman Radhakrishna, Vasant S Vaidya, Peter Nazareth and Victor Rangel-Ribeiro.

CHAPTER 8. GOA IN CREATIVE WRITING

As the blurb explains: "The sixteen stories in this special volume, mostly translated from Konkani and Marathi, delve into the depths of dignity-robbing poverty, the callousness of the landed gently, the heroic efforts of individuals to rise over shackling superstition and caste barriers and the inviolable hold of the ancestral village. This is a Goa far removed from the tourism brochure. And if there is a palm tree depicted in these stories, it carries a bonded coconut-plucker, thirsty for revenge. It does not sway."

In the Womb of Saudade: Stories of Goan Life
Lambert Mascarenhas
Rupa & Co.
Pp 239, Rs 80 (1994)
ISBN 81-7167-239-6.

Eleven stories, from an ex-editor who launched and ran the *Goa Today* magazine from the mid-1960s until the mid-1980s. The blurb says, "Characters are at once lovable and lively, drawn with a sure hand that speaks highly of his observation and imagination, this collection of short stories is a gift of Goa at its best...."

Modern Goan Short Stories
Luis Santa Rita Vas (Ed.)
Pp 173. Rs. 120 (2002)

Some 29 stories, in a reasonably-priced edition. The editor hopes that these short-stories are a kind of "biography of the Goan heart".

All the four major languages spoken and written in by Goans are represented here, "though not in proportion to their usage or output."

This book includes well-known writers — such as Armando Menezes, R.V. Pandit, Laxmanrao Sardesai, ManoharRai Sardesai, Alberto M. Rodrigues — and many more who "deserve to be better known".

Shattered Lives
Imelda Dias
Third Millennium, Pato, Panjim
Pp 166. Rs.175 (2003)

Six short stories set in Goa. And a glossary too.

Titles of some of the stories include Dying for the Goddess, The Rogue Landlord, Call Me 'Cecilia', I Love You 'Cat', Killing Rani, For Two *Kuddos* of Rice.

Its three-page glossary explains typically Goan words like *ambil, bai, beedi, till, tikha* and *zatra*, among others.

Old Cypress: Stories
Nisha da Cunha
Penguin.
Pp 198. Rs 65 (1991)

Mumbai-based author, b. 1935, taught at St Xavier's College in Mumbai, and directed several plays. She writes: "Many will think that this being a first book, the happenings in it are autobiographical. To which I can only say yes, and then, no."

The Village Home & Other Stories
J.P. D'Souza
Pp 141. Rs 75 (1998)

Stories that "try to give a picture of (Goa's) village life and the people who lived it." The author was at the University of Bombay. Also, a painter and music critic.

Dust and Other Stories from Goa
Heta Pandit Pp 231
Rs 250 (2002)

A collection of 20 short stories written over five years when the author was in Munnar (Kerala) and Varca (Goa). Cover by Mario de Miranda. Illustrations by architect-artist Sunita Dalvi.

Margaret Mascarenhas, author of the novel *Skin* comments: "Like a ventriloquist, whether in the first person or in the third, Pandit's narrator is credible as a man, woman, young or old. She crosses Indian class and cultural boundaries with amazing facility, and, frequently, with an ironic and unexpected humour."

Stray Stories *
R. V. Zuarkar
Goa Velha: Chamunda Publications
Pp 68. Rs 4 (1977)

Ten stories. Include ones with names like 'The Culprit', 'Happy Families', 'A Successful Marriage', 'My Cat', 'The Minister', 'My Profession', 'A Notorious Dacoit', 'Caste and Creeds', 'My God' and 'Power'.

Still Life and Other Stories *
Manuel C Rodrigues
The Coastal Observer, Bombay.
Pp 86. Rs 23 (1984)

Manuel C. Rodrigues, born in 1908 and whose roots get traced to Anjuna, was a poet, short-story writer, musician, composer, conductor and singer. He wrote in Konkani, English and Portuguese.

This book includes short-stories "some with an unmistakable Goan ambience". Siddharth College (Bombay) former head of the English Department Frank D'Souza offers a useful introduction. D'Souza likens the ending of 'Pranks' to the sudden twists of an O. Henry story. 'Orphans at Large' is described as based on Rodrigues' own impressions and experiences at Our Lady's Home at Dadar. 'Emmanuel' focuses on the customs and ceremonies which greeted a Goan new-born child in the past.

'Out in the Night' alludes to those who "braved the Goa night, steeped in superstitious fears, made furtively for the *zagor* – a truly pagan (sic) and ribald performance, where all local scandals were juicily exposed to a delighted, heterogeneous audience of young and old."

If anything, this shows how deeply the memories of home and Goa were embedded in migrants to Bombay decades ago. Undeniably, a lot of 'Goan' writing was crafted by the diaspora.

Tales From Goa *
Bertha Menezes Braganza
Bastora: Tipografia Rangel
Pp 221 (1991)

Writes ManoharRai L. SarDesai, of this book: "Bertha does not paint the golden sunshine of Goa's sandy beaches, nor the magnificence of its churches, nor the jasmin-like dreamy quality of its temples. Her Goa is not the paradise painted in dazzling colours. It is a place where selfishness has transformed man into an animal, and obscurantism clouded his clear vision. She depicts stark truth against the background of ignorance and poverty — the waves of words seething against the hard, naked rocks of reality."

Stories
Leslie de Noronha
Writers Workshop, Kolkata
Pp 76, np. (1966)

Ten short stories, earlier published in *The Illustrated Weekly, Reader's Magazine, The Century, Quest* and *Writers Workshop Miscellany*. Noronha, who came from a family of doctors and trained as one, opted for a life in writing.

HUMOUR, CARTOONS

One Sip At A Time
George Menezes
Better Yourself Books, Bombay

Pp 296. Rs 45 (1988)
ISBN 81-7108-063-4.

Light essays, some 95 in all, by a humour-writer with strong Goan roots. The author was a Squadron Leader in the Indian Air Force, a diplomat in Paris, and a human resources manager and trainer. Some of the essays have Goan themes. Others are suffused with the Goan world-view. See georgemenace.com

Goa With Love
Mario Miranda
M&M Associates, Surya, Reis Magos. (2001)

This book comprises drawings and text by the noted cartoonist Mario Miranda. It has been edited by Bal Mundkur, and design by Rishaad de Miranda.

Based on his cartooning in the mainstream media in the commercial capital of Mumbai, the book comes from a popular and widely-known cartoonist who was awarded the Padma Shri in 1988 and the Padma Bhushan in 2002.

Miranda has regularly been published in *The Times of India* and other newspapers in Mumbai, including *The Economic Times*. He is seen as having earned his popularity with his works published in *The Illustrated Weekly of India*.

Miranda's site says: "Nobody is better equipped to capture vignettes of Goan life than Mario Miranda." Wikipedia also notes that editor Manohar Shetty has praised the prominent cartoonist for "his eye for detail, his skills as a draughtsman, and the total absence of malice."

Other publications from Mario include *Laugh It Off by Mario* (IBH, Rs 6, 1974), *Sketchbook, A Little World of Humour*.

Architect Gerard da Cunha recently published the cartoonists life works in a tastefully-produced book simply called *Mario de Miranda*. This contains work by Mario from the time he was in his teens.

How to be an Instant Goan
Valentino Fernandes
Diamond Publications, Panjim.
Pp 155 + viii.

Journalist Valentino Fernandes' entertaining take on various aspects of Goan life. The writing is light, entertaining and refreshing. Fernandes, who recently retired from the *Gomantak Times*, struggled for long years to get his work published, but didn't give up.

Once it was out, the book did surprisingly well – which goes to show that persistence pays... specially in the tiny world for Goa writers. Val was known for his humour columns in the local Press.

Goa Paradise Lost: Environmental Cartoons
Alexyz Fernandes
Pp 160. Rs 50

A collection of cartoons, most of which have appeared a decade earlier in local publications. Also by the same author: *Sportoons* (IBH, Bombay), *Howzzat!* (Marine Sports, Bombay), *O Humor Goez* (Humorgrafe, Lisboa).

KONKANI LITERATURE

A History of Konkani Literature
ManoharRai SarDesai
Sahitya Akademi, New Delhi
Pp 318. Rs 160. (2000)
ISBN 81-7201-664-6

The author of this book has argued elsewhere that it is tough to make a "complete, period-wise survey" of Konkani literature. The reason? This language is written in "at least four distinct regions – Bombay, Goa, Mangalore and Cochin – and in four different scripts – Devanagari, Roman, Kannada and Malayalam."

SarDesai (whose name has also been spelt as Sardessai) saw the preoccupation of Konkani writers at the time (1980s and 1990s) with "taking good literature to the masses... trying to blend the spoken language with the literary language forged by Shenoy Goembab and others, combining the vigour of the former with the beauty of the latter".

The Makers of Konkani Literature *
Antonio Pereira, SJ
Rs 10 (1982)

A prolific writer in Konkani, Jesuit priest Antonio Pereira gives some useful insights into the past. He divides Konkani writing into three 'schools' – the Franciscan, the Jesuit and the Modern.

In the third, the most relevant if only due to proximity, he lists Dr Cunha Rivara, Dr Jose Gerson da Cunha, Eduardo Jose Bruno de Souza, Dada Vaidya and two others, Mgr. Sebastião Rodolfo Dalgado, Shennoy Goembab, Joaquim Antonio Fernandes, Dr Mariano Jose Saldanha, Dr Jose Pereira, Prof Lurdino Rodrigues, Dr ManoharRai Sardesai, and Dr R. V. Pandit.

One of the appendices is on Konkani grammars and grammarians.

Kali Ganga
Mahabaleshwar Sail
Translated by Vidya Pai
NBT
Pp 261. Rs 80 (2003)
ISBN 81-237-3857-9

Mahabaleshwar Sail (b 1943) joined the Indian Army at 17, and took part in the Goa operation, and also the Indo-Pak War. Beginning his literary work in Marathi, he later moved over to writing in Konkani.

Sail's novel is one of those mentioned in the relatively young tradition of novel-writing in Devanagari script Konkani.

IN PORTUGUESE

O Signo da Ira *
Orlando da Costa
4th Edition
Lisboa: Edições Temas da Actualidade, S.A.,
Pp 256 (1996)
ISBN 972-748-097-7

This is Orlando da Costa's first work as a novelist. It won him the Ricardo Malheiros Prize from the Lisbon Academy of Sciences.

Despite being banned by the censorship in place in Salazar's Portugal, it was hailed as one of the most outstanding neo-realist novels of its time. Published first in 1961 in Portugal, in a year that was fateful for Goa.

Writer Orlando António Fernandes da Costa (1929-2006) was Goan on his father's side, and Portuguese-French on his mother's. He was himself born in the capital of the former Portuguese colony of Mozambique, Lourenço Marques.

Costa spent his youth in Goa, and left for Lisbon at 18. He published his first work in poetry in 1951, *A Estrada e a Voz*. Later, he also worked on drama and romance.

He was in touch with many of the future leaders of the nationalist movements of the colonies, such as the MPLA, the FRELIMO and the PAIGC, and joined the Portuguese Communist Party in 1954. This was at a time when Oliveira Salazar still held a dictatorial grip over the Portuguese and the party was outlawed.

Incidentally, his son the lawyer and politician António Costa is a former minister, member of the European Parliament for the Socialist Party, and mayor of Lisbon. In July

2004, he was elected as one of the 14 Vice-Presidents of the European Parliament.

A Literatura Indo-Portuguesa *
Vimala Devi and Manuel de Seabra
Junta de Investigações do Ultramar, Lisbon.
Pp 367. 80$00 (1971)

This work in Portuguese offers an insight into another world, a world that rapidly fell into disuse after 1961.

It looks at Goa, the Portuguese, that language, the Church and Goan culture, early Goan writers in Portuguese, Indo-Portuguese writing, the cultural renaissance of Goa, Cunha Rivara, Tomas Ribeiro, and other related themes. It also touches on historiography of the 20th century, and poetry in the same period.

PLAYS

Goa and The Hungry Ones *
Two plays by Asif Currimbhoy
Suraiya Publishers
Pp 171 (1964)

Two plays, one linked to post-1961 Goa.

In it, Currimbhoy, a Parsi willing to take a stance few were in those times in a freshly-independent India, argues that the former Portuguese enclave's "historic take-over tarnished the moral image of India".

His story, which comes across as an allegory, is of "an Indian boy's love for a Goan girl, caught within the restraints of a half-Portuguese mother and her Portuguese lover".

Another edition which might be more accessible is *Goa: A Tragedy in Two Acts*. It was published in 1970 and 1982 by the Kolkata-based Writers Workshop (HB Rs 150, flexiback Rs 80, 132 pp ISBN 81-7189-272-8 and 81-7189-273-6 respectively).

The Rape of Goa: A Historical Tragedy in Five Acts
Patrick Ferdinand
Margao: Chowgule College,
Pp 72 Rs.100 N.d.

Probably published around 1998. M. N. Pearson writes: "The play deals with historical events, and claims to provide an account of how many Goans were converted to Christianity. The picture Mr Ferdinand paints is a bleak one indeed, yet his account is based on facts."

The author taught English language and literature in Aden, Bombay and Goa for 36 years. Ex-head of the Chowgule College, Department of English, now retired.

The Greater Tragedy.
Lambert Mascarenhas.
Goa: Lamas Publications
Pp 84. Rs 25 (1988)

A sequel to the much-better written *Sorrowing Lies My Land*, by an editor who played a crucial role in post-1961 Goa, first as joint-editor of *The Navhind Times*, and then running the *Goa Today* monthly for decades.

Mascarenhas says, "The purpose of this play is not to entertain." He explains that he wants to focus on "some unpublished facts" relating to the anti-colonial campaign with which he was associated with. Turns out a bit pedantic.

CHILDREN, YOUTH

Tales from Golden Goa
Anita Pinto
Pp 36 Rs 50 (1998)

Anita is a daughter of the Goa diaspora. More than that, she's a product of the still largely-unacknowledged melting-pot that makes up this small region. Her father, William

Coelho, was a history professor at St Xavier's College, Bombay. Her mother, Nur Fazul, an artist who studied at J.J. College of Art.

Anita is one of the then young team of ex-Xaviers and Sophia's alumni who returned to Goa in the 1970s. Environmentalist Claude and lawyer Norma Alvares, advocate Jos Peter D'Souza and cartoonist Alexyz Fernandes were among others. Agree with them or not, many went on to do things in Goa that wouldn't have happened without their being here.

Anita's book is devoted to her husband Nico. She writes: "'I have a dream', he said, 'to bring Goans back to Goa.' I hope my stories will realise a small part of his dream."

Her stories take us to a missing pig at Calangute, an adopted boy's Carnival, a kindly grandfather at Bastora, a runaway chicken at the Friday Market at Mapusa.

There are other typically Goan themes too: a sick child Raia who loves her *'kakon'* (typically Goan circular-shaped ring-bread), the age-old legend of St Francis Xavier's crab (which, interestingly, parallels the story of Hanuman and the squirrel), and Benaulim and its mosquitoes.

One tale takes us to a monsoon-hit village and the flooded fields of Saligao. There's another depicting a young boy's impatience for *nevreo* (the traditional pastry) at Ganesh Chaturthi, and yet another on a turtle at Palolem.

In Pinto's canvas, one comes across a wide range of Goan themes indeed: the San João feast, a fruit-stealing monkey, little Mehmood who helps at his father's shop in Vasco, and Kamla Maushi at Candolim.

How would the story of Goa be complete without mention of the emigration experience? So, there's granny Imelda Colaço eagerly awaiting her family's letter at her palatial house in Margao.

("Perhaps I should make a phone call tonight," thought Granny Imelda. "But I can't hear properly now and with their Canadian accent, I can't understand a word they say." She sighed.)

Other books that seek to take across Goan tales to children include:

- Goan Whoopee: Goan Tales For Children Anne de Braganca Cunha Pp 80. Rs 50 (1999). Neve Publishers, Gurgaon, Mumbai
- Tales of Goa * Pp 45 London (1997). Candy Rose Fernandes
- Folk Tales from New Goa, India * Sarah Davidson and Eleanor Phelps. in The Journal of American Folklore, Vol. 50, No. 195. (Jan. - Mar., 1937), Pp 1-51.
- Folklore in Salsette * Fr George Da Penha. Indian Antiquary, Nov.1887-Feb. 1893.

The Prince Of Camels
Cosme I Dias
Goa: Word Ventures
Pp 171. Rs 199 (India) $13.50 (2007)
ISBN 9788190480505

The Prince of Camels is a magical journey through the deserts of Arabia. The story is inspired by the congenial culture of the Arabian world (which the author says he experienced in Dubai, UAE).

The author is a former journalist who spent a longish stint taking care of *Herald*'s children's section published on the weekends.

Centered around a young Arab boy who is brought up by a race of magic camels called the Yassudis, its story takes the reader into the magical kingdom of Al Yassudi. There, you discover the human side of animals, and the animal side of human beings.

What's the story about? This is how it markets itself: "Any child deserves a home and loving parents! Yousuf, the infant Arab boy lost all that in a storm. Mossid, his father's favourite camel, is the only creature left alive, to protect him from the harsh Arabian desert." Well produced.

Alfie Alphonso: The search for the mystical crystal
Odette Mascarenhas
Pp 337. Rs. 175. (2006)

There are traces of Harry Potter in this story, and that's how it was described too at the time of its release.

Odette Mascarenhas' story is of a fairy godmother who enters the desolate world of a young Goan lad from the village of Aldona and transports him to the World of Magic where he tries to outwit the Dark Lord of Magic and his cohorts who are hell bent on preventing him from finding the Mystical Crystal.

This is Alfie Alphonso and his friends' second adventure. It has been described as, "Good magic to combat the evil forces." From the same author comes *Alfie Alphonso: The Blot on the Canvas (Pp 554.)* Besides this, the author has also, incidentally, penned the biography of a prominent chef from Goa *Masci: The Man Behind the Legend*.

Free From School
Rahul Alvares
Mapusa: Other India Bookstore
Pp 112. Rs 100 (1999)

When he was 16, Rahul Alvares — incidentally the son of environmentalist Dr Claude and lawyer Norma Alvares — stayed out of school for a year. During this time, he chose to unravel for himself the mysteries of nature's wonders reptiles, crocodiles, spiders, earthworms and turtles. This book is the story of Rahul's "real-life learning", away from the classroom and into new worlds.

Alvares' other book is *The Call of the Snake*. As its subtitle explains, this contains "real-life stories by a young snake-catcher from Goa". It was published in 2003 by the Other

India Press, and priced at Rs 110. 151 pages, ISBN 81-85569-57-6.

Maneka Gandhi reminds us in the foreword: "Goa has a wide variety of wildlife. A large number of bird watchers come to see the State's spectacular collection. Birds can be seen on outings early in the morning and even during the day. They can almost always be heard. I know this for a fact since I lived here during my formative years." She points out that snakes too can be "encountered almost everywhere" in Goa.

The Pepperns & Wars of the Mind
Frederika Menezes
Pp 173. Rs 200 (2003)

A whimsical tale of a world wholly of the imagination authored by a young Goan girl. Menezes has also authored *The Portrait – Rs. 100 Pp.81 (1998)*. Facing life as a spastic, she shares her pains, dreams and cheer with her readers.

Rebecca's Inheritance
Sushila Fonseca
Mumbai: Pauline Publications
Pp 189. Rs 55 (2002)

An adventure story set in Goa.

"When young Rebecca good-humouredly accepted her aunt's invitation to spend X'mas in Panmar, she never imagined that the short trip to scenic Goa was in reality to be the longest journey in her life. Trustingly, she compiled with her autocratic aunt's manipulations, only to find that life in the sleepy village of Panmar was full of treacherous undercurrents that threatened to destroy her very existence."

The author is a Margao-born practising pathologist in Goa. She schooled in Kenya, continued her education in Bombay, and has an MD in Pathology.

CHAPTER 8. GOA IN CREATIVE WRITING

■ Other books set in Goa include *The Sea Bird* by Mangala Anaveker Pp 84. Rs 100 (2001), and Surekha Panandikar's *The Bridge At Borim* Pp 79. Rs 14 (1999). This is a story of the exploits of a young boy, Jose, during the run-up to 1961, and the campaign to oust the Portuguese.

MISCELLANEOUS

Govapuri
Manohar Shetty (Ed)
Pp 120 (approx) Rs 20 each

Govapuri is a periodical from the now State-managed Institute Menezes Braganza, focussing on different aspects of Goan life. Topics it covered included essays and memoirs, heritage, planning and humour.

The humour volume, for instance, contains the "first ever English translation of an almost forgotten book" – *Jacob e Dulce*. Incidentally *Jacob e Dulce: Sketches from Indo-Portuguese Life* by Gíp (João da Costa) has also been published by the Sahitya Akademi of New Delhi (2004, pp 196, ISBN 81-260-1968-9) after being translated by Alvaro Noronha da Costa.

This was set in the 1890s. It includes Margao colloquialisms and was thought un-translatable. For instance, it mentions news-reports like "100 sausages stolen from Chandor shop". It also has Mario Miranda's early illustrations published over five decades ago in a 'Loutulensis League' souvenir!

Series editor Manohar Shetty is a journalist, editor and poet, who formerly edited *Goa Today* (1987-1993), three collections of poems, and Ferry Crossings (listed elsewhere here). Available at the Institute Menezes Braganza's first floor office above Panjim's Central Library. Also from some bookshops (e.g., OIBS at Mapusa).

Yes Ministerji
Carmo D'Souza
Calangute: Agnelo D'Souza
Pp 74. Rs 75 (2001)

Based on a series of articles that appeared in a local newspaper, the *Weekender*, between 1993-1995. Modified to make it comprehensible to the present-day reader, explaining events that unfolded in Goan politics then.

Ministerji, says the author, was conceived as a funny character, who would imitate, exaggerate, and ridicule real-life ministers of the last decade of 20th century Goa.

It features issues like the Konkan Railway protests, the 'Easter Episode' (the Governor sacking a chief minister at his "pleasure"), the Sea Transporter marooned on the Sinquerim coast and threatening it with oil pollution during the World Environment Day June 5, 1994 cyclone, illegal *matka* or two-digit gambling, political instability and more.

A Day in Goa (Ek Dis Goy'am) *
Folk operetta in English and Konkani
Basilio Magno, Frankfurt/m 1978

Songs include The Rock of Portugal, Heut ist Sontag (Sunday's A Day for Pray'r), Happy Birthday Jesus (Grüss Dich Jesus), Mog Mog Mog (Come, Love, Come), White Girl Valerie, Meu Portugal.

Dedicated to Gen. Manuel António Vassalo e Silva. "The last and most loved Portuguese Governor-General of Goa, Damao and Diu. He had in his hands to let Goa be destroyed...."

Magno has been active on in cyberspace for quite some time now, and he is the man behind the Proud To Be A Goan song, that has become an unofficial anthem of sorts for diaspora communities scattered across the globe.

Goa Freaks: My Hippie Years in India *
Cleo Odzer
NY: Blue Moon Books.
Pp 335. Np. (1995)
ISBN 1-56201-059-X

Not really fiction, but a well-narrated if glamourised account of the hippy years in Goa. The author escaped death from drugs in Goa, returned to the US, cleant-up, did her PhD, only to come back to Goa and pass away earlier this decade. She has a fan-following in cyberspace. See the group celebrating her life at http://groups.yahoo.com/group/Cleo_Odzer

A Spoke In the Wheel
Amita Kanekar
HarperCollins India
Pp 447. Pb. Rs 395 (2005)

The author is a Mumbai-based Goan, who teaches architectural history and comparative mythology. This is "a novel about the Buddha", and is slotted by its publishers as historical fiction.

Set in 256 BCE, some three centuries after the death of the Buddha, it revolves around a monk, Upali who is embittered by the terrible battle of Kalinga. Upali hates Emperor Ashoka, as also the war which made him overlord of the whole of India. Yet, Ashoka entrusts this very monk to put the Buddha's life and teachings down for posterity.

Kanekar's story is powerfully written and excellently narrated; her work earned her positive feedback from the mainstream media.

For instance, this is what *The Hindu* had to say: "... the book draws from Indian history to such good effect that one can't help wondering if things actually did happen this way.... Another interesting aspect of the book is the dismantling of each legend associated with the Buddha.... Life in the Magadhan empire is also portrayed with an eye to historical accuracy. Quotes from Ashokan edicts – which we knew of as history but couldn't really relate to – now come alive with a new imagery...."

The Moor's Last Sigh
Salman Rushdie
Vintage Books, London
Pp 434, UKP 7.99 (2006)
ISBN 798-0-099-59241-9

Moraes 'Moor' Zogoiby is a 'high-born crossbreed', the last surviving scion of a dynasty of Cochinese spice merchants and crime lords. Goa figures tangentially in the writing of Salman Rushdie here.

CYBERLINKS

Wikipedia's work-in-progress page on Goan writing is at: http://en.wikipedia.org/wiki/Goa_literature

It touches on topics such as: the early roots of Goan writing; writing by Goans in other languages; Goan writers; Indo-Portuguese writers, Konkani writing; resources for, and about, Goan writers; bibliography; sources; a 'see also' section; and external links.

As with other pages of the *Wikipedia*, feel free to edit and improve this text here.

Check http://openlibrary.org/ and do a search for Goa there. You'll be surprised by the number of books that show up, and you can even edit and add your own favourites!

Finally, here are a couple of blogs that have been promising to deal with Goa-related books and reviews:
- http://goabooks.wordpress.com/
- http://goabookreviews.blogspot.com

Finding Goa, via Arizona (an interview)

FROM the desert state of Arizona in the U.S., a researcher was drawn to the printed word emerging from this small region called Goa. DONNA YOUNG tells FREDERICK NORONHA what made her look at the literature of this distant land, and why she found Goan writing (primarily in English, which she studied) to be interesting.

From Arizona to Goa is a long distance. How did you get interested in the literature of this small region?

Actually I grew up in Atlanta, Georgia and moved to Arizona recently. As a small child I lived in a neighborhood of many Cuban refugees. I learned Spanish and became interested in Latin America. I pursued this interest and majored in Spanish at the Georgia State University.

Then, I went on to get a Masters in Spanish in California. I was not happy with the Doctorate programs at any of the universities in languages. I felt that they emphasized too much on literary analysis. I wanted to analyze literature according to the people who wrote it and how they were influenced by their history and society, rather than what metaphors, similes, and symbolism there were.

So, I decided that I would have to switch departments and went into history instead.

At Georgia State when I was taking some background

classes, I decided that it would be fun to branch out and take other areas instead of Latin America alone. I took classes on Africa, the Middle East, and South Asia.

The South Asian professor, James Heitzman, convinced me that I would be the ideal person to do research on Goa. He explained that Goa had been a Portuguese colony and it wouldn't be hard to learn Portuguese. True, it was quite different than what I had done in the past, but I do love to learn new things.

I went ahead and applied to graduate school there and did my thesis under his direction. Dr. Heitzman liked my idea of using literature to analyze the people, their history, and culture, and felt that I had the background that most students didn't have for combining those fields.

How does Goan writing compare with that from other 'foreign' cultures you've encountered?

In some ways, Goan writing in English is very different from Latin American writing. A lot of Latin American writing has a great deal of magical realism, whereas Goan literature has only a small amount.

I know the book *Skin* by Margaret Mascarenhas, and *Dust* by Heta Pandit has it, but most Goan literature doesn't. Goan literature tends to focus on history and culture. It's like looking through a mirror and seeing the past.

You can feel the issues of colonialism, the struggle for independence, and the clashes in deciding which language should be the State language. It does remind me of Mexican literature, in the way that Mexican literature gives you the feeling that you are re-living the Revolution. It provides a great deal of insight into Mexican culture. Of course, I haven't read any literature in Konkani or Marathi so I don't know if that literature is different.

What do you see as the strong points, and weak ones, of Goan writing in English?

I think that Goan literature is just starting to blossom.

The first strong point is that there are some very good writers.

Another is that when you read this literature, you get a strong sense of what it is to be Goan. There is a strong sense of the Goan Identity. The third strong point is more Goan literature is being published. I had a hard time keeping up with all of the new literature that was coming out. I finally had to cut it off and start writing.

As I see it, on the other hand, some writers aren't fully developed yet. As a writer, I know it takes time to develop that maturity. The reason I say this is because, in some of the literature, the characters are one-dimensional, the dialogue seems stilted, and plots need more developing.

Also, while this literature is interesting, it is mainly interesting to Goans. It would be wonderful if more writers could write literature that would have a broader appeal. That way, people who aren't Goan would be able to relate to Goa and their literature would be better known around the world.

The third weakness that I can see is that Goan literature isn't well known outside of Goa, with the exception of Goans who are abroad.

I had a terrible time trying to find sources for my research. I didn't find any Goan literature in my university library, and only found a handful of literature through an inter library loan.

The next thing I tried was having a friend's brother, who lives in Mumbai, order books for me by phone. He then sent them to me through a relative who was flying to the US. That helped, but I really needed more sources. Finally, I went to Goa and bought out almost all of the bookstores!

I do think that broader exposure would greatly help Goan writers because it would enable them to grow through an unbiased criticism of their work.

From all you read, which work impressed you the most? Why?

There were two books that I enjoyed the most.

The first was *Skin* by Margaret Mascarenhas. Maybe it's my past Latin American studies that drew me to it. But I feel that it has universal appeal. A lot of people can relate to a character who is trying to discover who she really is.

Another book that I loved was *Tivolem* by Victor Rangel-Ribeiro. I loved his sense of humour and the different characters in the book. There were a lot of people in his book that everyone has known in their lives — such as the town thief, the snooty rich lady, the newly rich who flaunt their wealth, and the local priests.

Tell us more about your work on this topic.

This research was for a Masters of Arts in South Asian history at the Georgia State University. I started my degree in 1998, but did not start researching my thesis until 2001.

In 2001, I went to Portugal to study Portuguese, then I returned to the US and started my research. In 2002, I went to Goa and finished my research there. It took me until December of 2005 before I finished writing.

It took me a long time because of several factors, one is that I have health problems, the other is that I wanted to make sure that I was writing a true depiction of the subject matter.

As for the number of works that I read, there were probably at least a couple of hundred. I didn't read just literature. I also read anthropology, sociology, history, travel and political science books about Goa. I read anything that I could get my hands on, with the exception of books in Konkani and Marathi.

I tried to read books in Portuguese and could figure out some of it, but not all. I also read newspapers, magazines and (cyberspace-based) message boards. Anything that would give me insight about the people and the culture.

Many people helped me with my project. The first person to help me was my thesis advisor Dr. James Heitzman.

He has several books and many articles published about India. He also was my editor and didn't hesitate to tell me when my work was not up to par. Dr. David McCreery, a specialist in Latin American history, also read and critiqued my thesis.

As for Goans who helped, my first contact was author Victor Rangel-Ribeiro. He advised on sources to read, gave me lots of suggestions and let me interview him as well as graciously setting it up for me to stay with his sister, the late Dr. Camila Ribeiro da Costa, and her husband Frank. Their knowledge and contacts were invaluable.

Author and professor Peter Nazareth at the University of Iowa also helped me a great deal by suggesting sources and answering questions.

In Goa, I also met with writer Margaret Mascarenhas and we discussed her work, in particular her book *Skin*. I also received assistance from Prajal Sakhardande at Dhempe College, who gave me a personal tour of Goa and answered all of my questions.

So many people helped me with this research. I couldn't have done it without them.

So, did you enjoy it? Or was wading through all those pages tiring?

I love to read! Reading was the easiest and most enjoyable part of the research. What was tiring was the writing. I had serious writer's block and really struggled to get it down on paper. Finally I checked myself into a hotel room and away from everyone, and I then got it written.

Tell us about your preferences in world literature, and reading?

I think it's obvious that I love Latin American literature. Mario Vargas Llosa and Gabriel Garcia Marquez are two of my favorites. But I also love mysteries.

Lately, I have been reading Tony Hillerman's books about two Navajo — a Native American tribe here in Arizona — tribal police officers who solve murders. Now that I live in Arizona, I am trying to learn more about the Native American tribes here. I enjoy reading books that broaden my horizons.

Tell us about yourself.

I enjoy other fields too such as history, anthropology and sociology. Well, you know I love to read and I read all types of books, fiction and non-fiction. I also have an interest in textiles and fiber arts. I really enjoy learning about different people's costumes and types of daily dress, both historical and modern day.

I went crazy in India with all of the gorgeous *saris* and *salwar kameezes*. I think I bought a dozen or so outfits to take home and I wear them proudly here in Arizona. As for my work, I have joined a writer's association here and I am learning about the business end on how to get published. In the future I want to return to Goa and do research on women in Goan history.

After having done it, what do you see as the unfinished work – which others need to take up, related to Goan writing?

I really wish someone would write a complete history of Goa. That would be great! I felt like I had to read a dozen books to get all of that information.

As for literature, how about a good mystery? That would be intriguing and it could include a lot of Goan culture. And maybe someone could do a literary analysis that includes Konkani and Marathi works. I really wished I could have read Konkani or Marathi literature, or at least had them in translation.

Index

A History of Konkani Literature, 100
A Kind of Absence, 97
Abbas, K.A., 42, 96
Achebe, Chinua, 75
Africa, 49, 71, 78–80, 84–86, 94
Alentejo, 46
Algarve, 46
Amonkar, Sudha, 66
Angela's Goan Identity, 35–39, 41, 58, 97
Angle, Prabhakar, 57, 96
Angola, 49
Archives in Panjim, vii
assimilados, 55
Ataide Lobo, Jorge, 45, 99
Australia, 26, 30, 78
Azores, 37

Back to the Village, 73, 74, 97
Bahrain, 78
bhatkar, 87
Black Skin White Masks, 40, 98

Boman-Behram, B.K., 43, 97
Bombay, 20, 26, 44, 46–48, 56, 61, 73, 76, 77, 86, 96–99
Botelho, Remigio, 79, 80, 97
Boyer, M., 68
British India, 59
British rule in India, 58
British rule in India, 72

Canada, 26, 30, 78
caste, 21, 42, 61, 64, 82, 84, 100
Christians, 21, 36–38, 56–58, 70, 78, 126
Christianity, 21, 34
community, 62
converts, 23
Goan, 35
Goan ties with other Christians, 78
heritage, 97

INDEX

language of worship, 56
Mallaca as a major centre, 71
migrants, 56
name, 35, 50
population in Goa, 21
Coelho, George, 101
Coimbra, 38, 46
Correia Afonso, John, 72
Couto, Maria Aurora, 57, 97
Cyber Voices, 68

D'Souza, Carmo, 35, 36, 58, 97
D'Souza, J.P., 73, 75, 76, 97
Daman, 25, 59
Dantas, Norman, 97
Danvers, Frederick C., 97
Dhempe College, vii
Diaspora, 29, 78, 82, 86, 89, 92, 94, 95
Diu, 25, 59
Drucker, Margaret, 58, 59, 98
Dust and other Short Stories from Goa, 77, 100

England, 26, 47, 86, 94
English, 27, 30, 38, 45, 55–59, 67–70, 74, 77, 82, 91, 94

Faces of Goa, 33, 35, 99
Faleiro, Luizinho, 63, 98
Fanon, Frantz, 40

Ferry Crossing: Short Stories from Goa, 62, 100

gauponn, 72
Glad Seasons in Goa, 76, 101
Goa and Ourselves, 43, 97
Goa Concepts and Misconcepts, 57, 96
Goa Congress Committee, 34
Goa Today, 65, 99
Goa University, 52, 73
Goa's Struggle for Freedom, 101
Goa, by Louise Nicholson, 100
Goa: A Daughter's Story, 124
Goa: An Economic Update, 96
Goa: Continuity and Change, 97, 98, 100, 101
Goa: Cradle of my Dreams, 98
Goa: Facts versus Fiction, 60, 61, 100
Goa: Transformation of an Indian Region., 99
Goacom.com, 98
Goan
    adopting a third identity, 70
    emigration, 87
    exile, 89

identity, 50
literature, 50, 87, 91
separate identity, 19
women, 88
Goan Overseas Digest, 98
Gomes, Olivinho J.F., 98
Great Britain, 30
Gulf, 87

Henry, Joseph K., 41, 98
Hindu, 78
Hindus, 21, 37, 56–58, 61
Albuquerque policy, 34
and education, 57
and language, 56
and the Inquisition, 23
and the Portuguese, 22
caste, 64
converts to Christianity, 21
forefathers as, 37
Goa Hindu Association, 96
history, 92
in the New Conquests, 24
influences, 30
language, 62, 66
language and identity, 70
percentage of population, 21
population in Goa, 20
pre-Portuguese Hinduism, 88
rituals, 23
temples, 23
ties outside Goa, 78
Vijayanagar empire, 22
Hobgood, John, 28
Homework, 44, 100

Indian, 38, 42–44
Into the Mainstream, 100

Journal of South Asian Literature, 99, 100

Kamat, Sharmila, 64, 99
Karmali, Naguesh, 67
Kenya, 79
Konkan region, 61
Konkani, 23, 26, 27, 29, 30, 33, 36, 39, 40, 53–70, 72, 87, 89, 91, 96–100
Konkani Mai Ascends the Throne, 99
scripts, 56, 62
theatre, 70
Konknni My Mother Tongue, 65
Kuwait, 26, 78

Larsen, Karin, 33, 34, 69, 99
Leitao, Lino, 70, 82, 83, 99
Liberation, 51, 77
Liberation: A Novel, 45, 99

Lisbon, 46, 47, 49
Luso-Marathi schools, 57

Madeira, 37, 94, 95, 97, 99
Maharashtra, 20, 26, 54, 56, 59, 60, 62–65, 67–69, 91
Maharashtrawadi Gomantak Party, 59, 63, 65
Malacca, 71
Mango Mood, 64, 99
Mangoes and Chappaties, 58
Marathi, 26, 27, 31, 33, 36, 37, 53–70, 91, 99
Margao, 25, 71
Maria, 42, 43, 96
Mascarenhas, Lambert, 40, 50, 99
Mascarenhas, Margaret, 49, 50, 99
Mascarenhas, Telo de, 46–49, 98
Mayekar, Gopalrao, 65
Michael Lobo Publishers, 97
Middle East, 77
Modern Goan Short Stories, 100
Muslims, 21, 22, 58
My Goa: An Autobiography, 63, 98

Naik, Pundalik N., 75, 97, 99
Naik, Vinayak, 66, 99

Narayan, Rajan, 60, 99
Nazareth, Peter, vi, 28, 30, 70, 85, 88, 99
New Conquests, 60
Newman, Robert S., 54, 64, 78, 99
Nora Secco de Sousa, 64, 98
Noronha, Frederick, vi, vii
Noronha, Leslie de, 40, 83, 98
Noronha, Percival, vii

Of Umbrellas, Goddesses, and Dreams, 99, 100
Official Language Act, 91
Old Goa, vii
    Velha Goa, 71
On A Goan Beach, 79, 97
On the Mango and the Tamarind Tree, 98
Opinion Poll, 26, 59
Orientalism, 27
Other India Press, 96, 97

Pai, Vidya, 97
Panaji (Panjim), vii, 20, 25, 52, 71
Pandit, Heta, 77, 87, 100
Pearson, M.N., 100
Peres da Costa, Suneeta, 44, 100
Persian Gulf, 80
Portugal, 24–26, 36, 38, 71

Portuguese, 44, 46, 48, 51, 54, 58, 71, 72, 88
  citizenship, 51
  departure of, 79
  domination, 30
  education, 38
  enclaves, 25
  identity, 43, 90
  in fiction, 36
  language, 39, 77, 90
  speakers in Goa, 54
  troops, 25
  writing about, 27
Priolkar, A.K., 32, 33, 60–62, 64, 100
Pune, 56

Rachol Seminary, vii
Rangel-Ribeiro, Victor, vi, 52, 70, 80, 100
Ressurge, Goa, 47, 49
return from exile, 30, 73, 77, 78
Rodrigues, Eusebio L., 78, 86, 89, 100
Rubinoff, Arthur, 55, 56, 100
Rubinoff, Janet, 100

Sahitya Akademi, 64
Said, Edward, 26, 28
Sakhardande, Prajal, vii
Salazar, Antonio Oliveira de, 48, 49, 58
Santa Rita Vas, Luis, 54, 100

Sardessai, Manohar Hirba, 66
Sardessai, ManoharRai, 28, 72, 100, 129
Shetty, Manohar, 62, 100
Shirodkar, P.P., 101
Shivdas, N., 67
Simoes, Frank, 76, 101
Skin, vii, 49, 50, 99
Sorrowing Lies My Land, 39, 40, 99
Souza, Teotonio R. de, 29
Stephens, Father Thomas, 66

Thanks to the Goa Bus System, 82
The Construction of a Political Community: Integration and Identity in Goa, 100
The Denationalization of Goans, 34, 60, 95, 98
The End of Exile, Or, Why Should Goans Read Goan Literature?, 99
The General is Up, 85, 86, 99
The Goa Action, 99
The Greater Tragedy, 50, 99
The Gulf, 26, 87
The Indian Ocean (Seas in History), 100
The Life of Jesus, 66

INDEX

The Mango and the Tamarind Tree, 40, 41, 83, 84, 98
The Portuguese in India, 97, 100
The Transforming of Goa, 96, 97, 101
The Upheaval/Acchev, 27, 75, 97, 99
The Village Home and Other Stories, 76, 97
Things Fall Apart, 75
Thoughts on Exile, 86
Tivolem, 80, 81, 100, 107, 161
traditional Goan society, 80

United Kingdom, 78
United States, 30, 49, 50, 78, 90, 91, 98

Vasco, 71
Village Goa, 98

Wagle, Narendra, 101
When the Mango Trees Blossomed, 46, 98

Xavier Center for Historical Research, vii